CAR INVESTIGATIONS

By Kelly E. Riddle

KELMAR GLOBAL

Private Investigations and Security

Dewayne—
Keep the faith brother!.

Kelly E Riddle

WED, 08/17/2016
@ World Investigator/IALI
Conference & Seminar
LaTorretta Lake Resort & Spa
Montgomery, TX

Published by
Kelly E. Riddle
2553 Jackson Keller, Suite 200
San Antonio, TX. 78230
(210) 342-0509

TABLE OF CONTENTS

UNDERSTANDING CAREGIVERS
Chapter One

Most of us relate caregivers as individuals with a high degree of ethics, compassion and love for their fellow man. Your mind wants to conjure up a Mother Teresa[1] comparison who of course won the Noble Prize for her work in caregiving. In its truest form we are told by Jesus Christ in the second Commandment to "love they neighbor as thy self."[2] While it is true that the majority of caregivers strive for the ultimate goal of helping better the lives of those under their charge, this book deals with the few among us that deviate from the norms of mankind.

We must first understand and define what and who a caregiver is and their functions. In the general sense, a caregiver is anyone that contributes towards the welfare of a sick, elderly or incapacitated person. While some definitions attempt to make a distinction between those who are paid and those who are not, for our purposes we will stick to those who are tasked with providing care as a professional. This will include in-home nursing, adult and child daycare facilities, hospitals and assisted living facilities.

There are many definitions[3] for caregiver including the following:

1. An individual, such as a physician, nurse, or social worker, who assists in the identification, prevention, or treatment of an illness or disability.

2. An individual, such as a parent, foster parent, or head of a household, who attends to the needs of a child or dependent adult.

3. One who contributes the benefits of medical, social, economic, or environmental resources to a dependent or partially dependent individual, such as a critically ill person.

4. Any person, including a family member, who provides care or assistance to one who is ill.

Responsibilities of caregivers vary based on the age, physical and mental condition of the patient, sickness or disease and socio-economic status.

---

[1] http://www.nobelprize.org/nobel_prizes/peace/laureates/1979/teresa-bio.html
[2] Matthew 22:39
[3] http://medical-dictionary.thefreedictionary.com/Caregivers

Daycare centers are normally thought of in regards to children but there are adult daycare facilities where elderly or those with physical or mental conditions can go during the day to enjoy fellowship and stimulus from games or activities. The licensing requirements are not are strenuous as other medical facilities. The term "assisted living" has a wide spectrum of meanings when discussing their levels of care. The following is a list of the various types, levels and definitions associated with assisted living centers:[4]

24-hour Controlled Access	Some senior facilities have security systems that only allow authorized personnel into the buildings.
Accreditation Definition:	A designation or seal of approval given by an independent governing body that a community of service meets specific requirements as designation by the controlling body.
ACHCA Definition:	The American College of Health Care Administrators (ACHCA) is a non-profit professional membership association which provides educational programming, certification, and career development opportunities for care administrators.
Activities of Daily Living (ADLs)	Activities of daily living are typically defined as bathing, dressing, assistance with using the toilet, eating, moving around to perform daily

[4] http://www.seniorliving.org/library/definitions/

	life supporting tasks.
ADA (Americans with Disabilities Act)	The ADA was passed by Congress in 1980 to establish a comprehensive and clear prohibition of discrimination and the basis of a disability.
Adaptive / Assistive Equipment Definition:	An appliance, gadget or piece of equipment designed to assist users in self-care, leisure activities or work. This can include in-home elevators, special eating implements and walking aids.
Administration on Aging (AOA)	An agency of the U.S. Department of Health and Human Services that is an advocate agency for older persons (seniors) and their concerns at the federal level.
Administrator Definition:	Typically a licensed professional who has the overall responsibility of the day-to-day operations of a care community like an independent living assisted living or nursing home.
Adult Day Care Definition:	An organization that provides structured program for seniors including stimulation social activities. Many also provide rehab services for the elderly that are emotionally or physically disabled.
Adult Day Health Care Definition:	An organization that

	provides care and services in a residential health care facility or approved extension site, on an outpatient basis, under the medical direction of a physician. Services are in accord with a comprehensive assessment of care needs and individualized health care plan.
Adult Family Home Definition:	A facility that provides a private, home-like setting and serves a limited number of residents who receive care from live-in caretakers. These facilities are typically in a residential neighborhood and provides group meals, housekeeping and laundry. Services vary widely in these facilities, so check each location for specifics. (Also called Group Home, Board and Care Home, Residential Care Facility, Adult Foster Care and Personal Care Home.)
Advanced Directives Definition:	A written statement (often part of a will) of a senior's preferences and directions regarding health care. Advanced Directives are created to protect a person's rights even if he or she becomes unable to choose or communicate

	his or her wishes.
Advantage List Definition:	A list of healthcare service providers that agree to give particular insurance company policyholders a preset discount often included in long term care insurance.
Aging in Place Definition:	Aging is Place is a concept where seniors continue to live at home or with a family regardless of their mental and physical decline. This concept requires resources like in-home caregivers.
Alzheimer's Definition:	A progressive form of pre-senile dementia that is similar to senile dementia except that it usually starts in the 40s or 50s. The first symptoms are impaired memory which is followed by impaired thought and speech and finally complete helplessness. Alzheimer's is caused by a buildup of plaque in the brain that limits its ability to function.
Alzheimer's Care Center Definition:	A treatment center or facility that specializes in providing care for those with Alzheimer's disease. These facilities are geared towards supervision of the patient in a safe and controlled

	environment.
Ambulatory Definition:	The ability to walk and move freely without another person's assistance, not bedridden or hospitalized.
Activities of Daily Living (ADLs)	Area Agencies on Aging (AAA) is organization tries to help older persons and persons with disabilities live with dignity and choices in their homes and communities for as long as possible.
Assessment Definition:	An evaluation or test, usually performed by a professional life a physician to determine a person's mental, emotional, and social capabilities.
Assisted Living Definition:	A senior lifestyle that provides a combination of housing, personalized supportive services and health care designed to meet the needs of seniors who need help with activities of daily living.
Certified Home Health Care (CAN)	A certified nursing assistant, who helps a nurse care for a patient including preventative, therapeutic, health guidance and/or supportive help to persons at home and/or at a senior housing facility
Congregate Housing Definition:	Similar to independent living but Congregate Housing may provide

	additional conveniences or supportive services like meals, housekeeping and transportation in addition to rental housing. A lower level of care than assisted living.
Continuing Care Retirement Community (CCRC)	A community that offers multiple levels of senior living, including independent living, assisted living, hospice and skilled nursing care. A CCRC will create long-term contract between the resident (frequently lasting the term of the resident's lifetime) and the community which offers a continuum of housing, services and health care system throughout the decline of the residence health. All the care options are commonly on one campus or site allow the resident to maintain friends and consistent activities even as their care need change.
Continuum of Care Definition:	Care services to assist individuals throughout a wide range to health care requirements. This may include Independent Living, Assisted Living, Nursing Care, Hospice, Home Care, and Community Based Services.
Convalescent Home Definition:	A common name for a

	skilled nursing facility
Custodial Care Definition:	Room, board and other personal assistance services including assistance with activities of daily living (ADLs) and taking medicine

You can see from the above that you will get a quick crash course on assisted living facilities if you are in the position to need one for a family member. I recommend that a person begins to acquaint themselves with this industry at the first sign or indication that a family may need one in the near future. The family most assuredly will run into resistance when introducing the concept to the potential assisted living candidate. Being educated on the topic in advance will allow you to discuss the topic in a more educated and responsible manner.

The duties of caregivers have a vast range depending on the nature of the care and the condition and needs of the patient. Some of these include:

- Running errands
- Helping with household chores (bedding, laundry, etc.)
- Assisting in paying bills
- Helping with skin conditioning
- Assisting in bathing
- Gentle massages
- Range of motion exercises
- Insuring adequate diet
- Assisting with eating
- Taking to doctor's appointments
- Maintaining regular dental, hearing and eyesight exams
- Insuring the patient stays hydrated
- Insuring medicine and vitamins are consumed
- Anything else that positively effects the quality of life

Initially the family may be able to utilize a part-time in-home caregiver who drops in 3-4 times a week to check on the person. During these visits the caregiver can observe the capabilities of the person to determine if they are still able to conduct daily activities such as bathing, laundry, minimal meal preparation and similar tasks. If dementia is suspected, the caregiver can gauge the status or progression of this disease. It is for these reasons that the same caregiver should be utilized whenever possible to enable the caregiver to have a basis in which to make assessments. The transition can then be made to a full-time in-home caregiver or to an assisted living facility.

In the past 12 months (2009), an estimated 65.7 million people in the U.S. have served as *unpaid* family caregivers to an adult or a child[5]. About 28.5% of the respondents surveyed reported being caregivers. The percentage of people who are caregivers does not appear to have changed significantly since 2004.

Figure 1: Estimates of Individual Caregiving Prevalence by Age of Recipient

Type of Recipient	Prevalence	Estimated Number of Caregivers
Overall	28.5%	65.7 million
Only child recipients	1.7%	3.9 million
Only adult recipients	21.2%	48.9 million
Both adult and child recipients	5.6%	12.9 million

-More than three in ten U.S. households (31.2%) report that at least one person has served as an unpaid family caregiver within the last twelve months, leading to an estimate of 36.5 million households with a caregiver present.

-Caregivers are predominantly female (66%). They are 48 years of age, on average.

-One-third take care of two or more people (34%).

-A large majority of caregivers provide care for a relative (86%), with over one-third taking care of a parent (36%).

-One in seven care for their own child (14%).

-Caregivers have been in their role for an average of 4.6 years, with three in ten having given care to their loved one for five years or more (31%).

Main Problem or Illness of Care Recipient Identified by Caregiver:

---

[5] http://www.caregiving.org/research/caregiving-research/general-caregiving

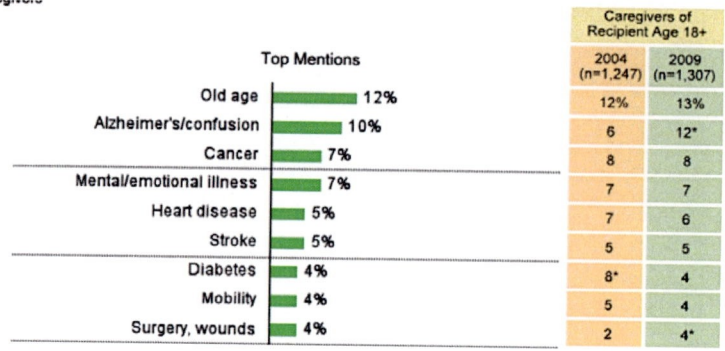

Top Mentions		Caregivers of Recipient Age 18+	
		2004 (n=1,247)	2009 (n=1,307)
Old age	12%	12%	13%
Alzheimer's/confusion	10%	6	12*
Cancer	7%	8	8
Mental/emotional illness	7%	7	7
Heart disease	5%	7	6
Stroke	5%	5	5
Diabetes	4%	8*	4
Mobility	4%	5	4
Surgery, wounds	4%	2	4*

On average, caregivers spend 20.4 hours per week providing care.

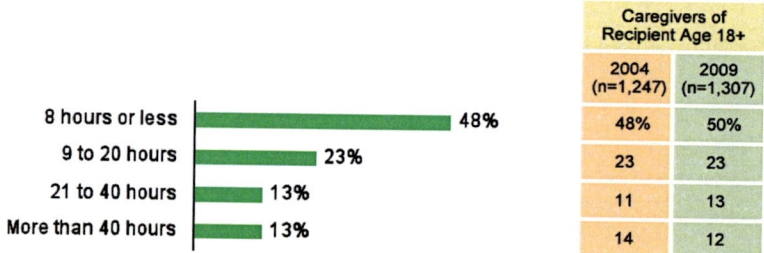

		Caregivers of Recipient Age 18+	
		2004 (n=1,247)	2009 (n=1,307)
8 hours or less	48%	48%	50%
9 to 20 hours	23%	23	23
21 to 40 hours	13%	11	13
More than 40 hours	13%	14	12

Again, these statistics are for "unpaid" caregivers who choose to provide this care in addition to working other jobs, taking care of their immediate family; all while trying to maintian some similance of joy in their life. What these figures do not provide is information related to strain on marriages and families, the caregiver's own health and financial stress.

Compare these statistics to paid nursing assistants:[6]

According to the National Clearinghouse on the Direct Care Workforce, direct-care workers provide an estimated 70 to 80 percent of the paid, hands-on long term care and personal assistance received by Americans who are elderly, chronically ill, or living with disabilities. These workers go by many names, but they fall into three main occupational categories: nursing assistants (usually known as certified nursing assistants or CNAs), home health aides, and personal and home care aides.

According to a study by the American Health Care Association, annual

---

[6] http://www.clintmaun.com/index.php5?cID=265

turnover rates among the long term care industry are approximately 70 percent. In other words, two out of three nursing home or long term care workers leave their jobs in the course of a year.

Logically, this would tend to indicate stress at the workplace, poor working conditions and low pay. This is a current that runs through the industry and plays a major role in the ultimate neglect and abuse.

The wages (and the lack thereof) are a significant issue that contributes directly to neglect and abuse. The adage, "you get what you pay for" certainly applies in this situation. According to the U.S. Department of Labor[7], the following applies:

Summary

Quick Facts: Nursing Assistants and Orderlies	
2012 Median Pay ?	$24,400 per year $11.73 per hour
Entry-Level Education ?	See How to Become One
Work Experience in a Related Occupation ?	None
On-the-job Training ?	See How to Become One
Number of Jobs, 2012 ?	1,534,400
Job Outlook, 2012-22 ?	21% (Faster than average)
Employment Change, 2012-22 ?	321,200

While the number of jobs available and the outlook for jobs is promising, getting a good quality of people for those positions are an obstacle. The average pay in 2012 for a nursing assistant or orderly was only $24,400 a year. Ask yourself if you would work shift work, clean bodily fluids, aggressively attend to bedsores and be under appreciated for $24,000 a year! There are certain things in life where paying a top-shelf fee is worth it. This happens to be one of them.

---

[7] http://www.bls.gov/ooh/Healthcare/Nursing-assistants.htm

UNDERSTANDING WHAT WENT WRONG
Chapter Two

On the extreme side are those associated with Adolph Hitler.[8] While he certainly could not have been considered a caregiver, there were those medical professionals under his command who strayed grossly from their professional and ethical oaths to not only use humans as human guinea pigs but were involved in documented torture.[9] What is intriguing is how highly educated, highly trained medical professionals could be coerced into such deviant behavior. *Again, for the purposes of this book we will deal with those individuals requiring a certification or licensing as a professional caregiver.*

So what causes a person to abuse other people? Some were abused and they are re-creating what they "know". Many have a need to be dominant because that is the only method they know to be heard or feel important. Stress within their own life causes them to lash out. Being in a type of mid-life crisis where they find themselves at a low paying, go nowhere job may also be a contributing factor. According to statements overheard, some thoughts vocalized by caregivers include[10]

Some Non-Angelic Caregiver Thoughts

    1. I have no life of my own and I'm sick of it.

---

[8] http://en.wikipedia.org/wiki/Adolf_Hitler
[9] http://en.wikipedia.org/wiki/Nazi_human_experimentation
[10] http://www.agingcare.com

2. Mom acts like my boss even when it comes to what I eat.

3. How much longer can I keep this up? There is no light at the end of this tunnel.

4. Dad has no clue what I give up to do this. He thinks his care is routine.

5. Everybody wants a piece of me – there's nothing of myself left for me.

6. I can't even take a bath without someone needing me.

7. Nothing I do pleases them – they are never happy.

8. I just want to scream, run away, hide somewhere, or change my identity.

9. Maybe if I just take all of Mom's sleeping pills I won't have to wake up to this again.

10. She is suffering so much. She's been half dead for months. Why can't she just let go and die?

According to Dr. Maryls Bratelli[11] the following actions contribute to caregiver's abuse:

What pushes caregivers over the edge?
- Behavior traits of the older person.
- The nature of the tasks that have to be performed on a daily basis.
- Frustration experienced by the care provider.
- The care provider's sense of isolation.
- Lack of services and/or other community support.
(Pritchard. 1996)

---

[11] http://www.ndsu.edu

There is individual abuse, where a resident or residents are hit, they are verbally abused, or have their money stolen or misused. One of the contributing factors is the administration of the facility. According to the study on Caregiver Abuse, Neglect and Exploitation[12] other contributing factors include:

Signs of Caregiver's Abuse

- Awaken residents too early in the morning.

- Does not provide flexibility in choice in the time of going to bed.

- Denies residents' opportunity for getting drinks and snacks.

- Limits choice and consultation about meals; the last meal being served too early.

- Refuses residents' personal possessions, furniture, telephone, TV, radio, etc.

- Has no procedure for washing, mending, and marking personal clothing.

- Provides too few toileting facilities.

- Does not help residents stay clean and tidy; does not provide underwear.

- Handles medical complaints poorly.

---

[12] http://www.ndsu.edu/ndsu/aging/caregiver/pdf/abuse/manual.pdf

In the United States, the 2010 Census recorded the greatest number and proportion of people age 65 and older in all of decennial census history: 40.3 million, or 13% of the total population. This "Boomer Generation" effect will continue for decades.[13]

America's Growing Elderly Population

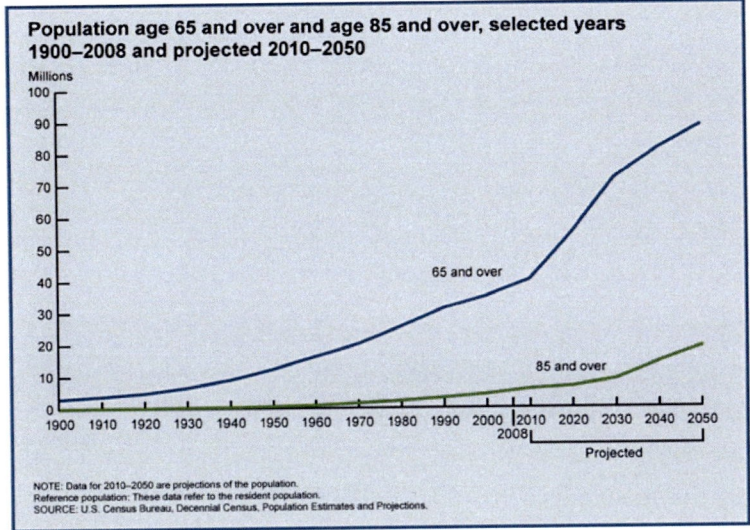

Looking at a specific segment of the population that should be the most quantitative segment of the populace gives us sketchy statistics. We simply do not know for certain how many people are suffering from elder abuse and neglect. It appears that female elders are abused at a higher rate than males and that the older one is, the more likely one is to be abused.[14]

Signs of elder abuse may be missed by professionals working with older Americans because of lack of training on detecting abuse. The elderly may be reluctant to report abuse themselves because of fear of retaliation, lack of physical and/or cognitive ability to report, or because they don't want to get the abuser (90% of whom are family members) in trouble.

According to the National Center on Elder Abuse, below is a sampling of findings that show what is known about the incidence and prevalence of elder abuse and neglect:

[13] U.S. Dept. of Commerce, U.S. Census Bureau. (2011)
[14] National Center on Elder Abuse

- The most recent major studies on incidence reported that 7.6%–10% of study participants experienced abuse in the prior year.[6,7] The study that found an incidence of 1 in 10 adults experiencing abuse did not include financial abuse.[8]

- Available data from state Adult Protective Services (APS) agencies show an increasing trend in the reporting of elder abuse.

- Despite the accessibility of APS in all 50 states (whose programs are quite different), as well as mandatory reporting laws for elder abuse in most states, an overwhelming number of cases of abuse, neglect, and exploitation go undetected and untreated each year.

- One study estimated that only 1 in 14 cases of elder abuse ever comes to the attention of authorities.[9] The New York State Elder Abuse Prevalence Study found that for every case known to programs and agencies, 24 were unknown.[10]

- Major financial exploitation was self-reported at a rate of 41 per 1,000 surveyed, which was higher than self-reported rates of emotional, physical, and sexual abuse or neglect.

Approximately 14 million U.S. adults aged 65 and over and 19 million U.S adults aged 18 to 64 have a disability. Unfortunately, some of these vulnerable adults are abused by family members, service providers, care assistants and others. This abuse places the victim's health, safety, emotional wellbeing, and ability to engage in daily life activities at risk.

Below is a sampling of research findings relating to abuse of adults with disabilities:

- Institutionalized adult women with disabilities reported a 33% prevalence of having ever experienced interpersonal violence (IPV) versus 21% for institutionalized adult women without disabilities.

- When considering lifetime abuse by any perpetrator, a sample of 200 adult women with disabilities indicated that 67% had experienced physical abuse and 53% had experienced sexual abuse.

- In a study of 342 adult men, 55% of men experienced physical abuse by any person after becoming disabled. Nearly 12% of these men stated they experienced physical abuse by a personal assistance service provider over their lifetime.

- In a comprehensive review of literature published from 2000–2010, lifetime prevalence of any type of IPV against adult women with disabilities was found to be 26–90%. Lifetime prevalence of IPV against adult men with disabilities was found to be 28.7–86.7%. It was concluded that, over the course of their lives, IPV occurs at disproportionate and elevated rates among men and women with disabilities.

How Many Long Term Care Facilities Are in the U.S.?

16,639 Nursing Homes with 1,736,645 beds
(NORS, 2010)

52,681 Board & Care Homes with 1,212,015 beds
(NORS, 2010)

How Many People Live in Long Term Care Facilities?

3.2 million Americans resided in nursing homes during 2008
(CMMS, 2009)

According to the National Center for Assisted Living (2008), **"more than 900,000 people nationwide live in assisted living settings."**

Who Lives in Long Term Care Facilities?

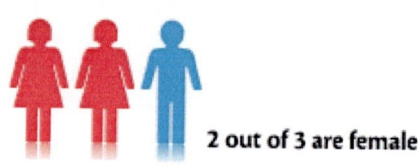

2 out of 3 are female

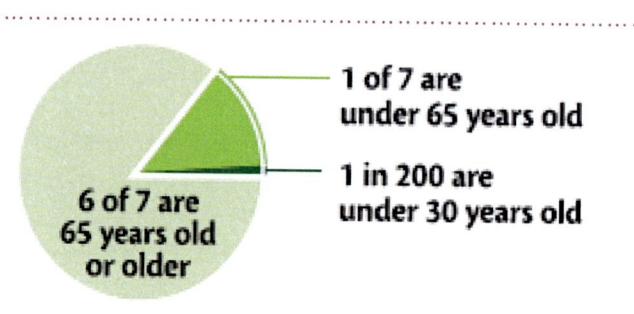

1 of 7 are under 65 years old

1 in 200 are under 30 years old

6 of 7 are 65 years old or older

How Prevalent Is Elder and Vulnerable/Dependent Adult Abuse?

- Over **50% of nursing home staff admitted to mistreating (e.g. physical violence, mental abuse, neglect) older patients** within the prior year in one study. Two thirds of those incidents involved neglect. (Ben Natan, 2010)

- One survey of certified nursing assistants (CNA) found that **17% of CNAs had pushed, grabbed, or shoved** a nursing home resident. **51% reported they had yelled** at a resident and **23% had insulted or sworn** at a resident. (Pillemer & Hudson, 1993)

- **7% of all complaints** regarding institutional facilities reported to long term care Ombudsmen **were complaints of abuse, neglect, or exploitation.** (NORS Data 2010)

- Nearly **1 in 3 U.S. nursing homes were cited for violations** of federal    standards that had potential to cause harm or that had caused actual harm to a resident during the two years 1999-2001. Nearly 1 out of 10 homes had violations that caused residents harm, serious injury, or placed them in jeopardy of death. (2001 U.S. House of Representatives Report)

- In a study of 2,000 interviews of nursing home residents, **44% said they had been abused and 95% said they had been neglected or seen another resident neglected.** (Broyles, 2000)

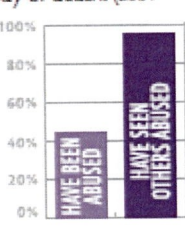

In the real world, in today's society, there are stories after stories depicting abuse. From children to the elderly you don't have to look far in the media to find examples:

Caregiver accused of using electric weapon on school children[15]

Posted: 11:02 a.m. Friday, Jan. 31, 2014

Kissimmee, Fla. —

A caregiver in Kissimmee was arrested on child abuse charges after she was accused of using an electric weapon to punish children, authorities said.

Investigators said a 9-year-old girl from Sunrise Elementary School told officials that whenever she and her brothers, aged 7 and 8, got into trouble their caregiver Letina Smith would "come up to them with an electrical weapon and activate it and touch them with it, and that it hurt very much and they were afraid of it."

The children claimed that Smith, 41, would use a pink rectangular-shaped, two-pointed device that had electricity flowing between the points and

---

[15] http://www.wftv.com/news/news/local/caregiver-accused-using-electric-weapon-school-chi/nc8PH/

would touch them with it when they misbehaved, police said.

A police report said the children would be put into an "electric chair" if they got into trouble.

Police said Smith admitted having an electric weapon and said she would activate it and hold it a few inches from the children, but would not touch them with it.

Caregiver Accused of Financial Elder Abuse and Murder in Presumed Death of San Diego Senior Citizen

Posted on August 12, 2013 by Ingrid Evans

ATTORNEY NEWSLETTER[16]

A caregiver has been charged with murder and a special circumstance allegation of murder for financial gain in connection with the presumed death of an 89 year-old senior victim in San Diego. Gerald Rabourn, the senior victim, disappeared in October of 2010. His body has never been found, but he has not been heard from and there is no evidence that he is still alive. San Diego elder abuse attorneys say that this is a particularly egregious case of financial elder abuse that ended in tragedy.

The caregiver was hired through a senior care service to provide care to Carolyn Rabourn, Gerald's wife. Carolyn Rabourn died of cancer in September of 2010. After that, Gerald Rabourn trusted the caregiver with his financial affairs. Within days of the death of his wife, the financial elder abuse began when caregiver began to drain the bank accounts of Gerald Rabourn and convert his assets for her use.

Rabourn's daughter stated that she tried to convince him to move to the Midwest in October of 2010, but he wanted to stay in his house and live with the caregiver. After that, the caregiver allegedly gave family members inconsistent reports regarding Rabourn's location after his wife's death. According to police, there was an abrupt end to Rabourn's contact with his family, cell phone use, and financial activity after October 21, 2010. Subsequent to that date, his signature was forged on a document to sell the family home and transfer the title of his car, according to police.

---

[16] http://www.evanslaw.com/caregiver-accused-of-financial-elder-abuse-and-murder-in-presumed-death-of-san-diego-senior-citizen/

Rabourn's daughter said that her father was financially sound and had told her that she was to inherit his entire estate. An attorney she spoke with told her that her father and the caregiver had come to the office to change his will, but assured her that the caregiver could not get any of her father's money. She spoke to her father for the last time on October 19, 2010 but did not report him missing until February of 2011. She stated that the caregiver kept giving her reports on the whereabouts of her father during the interim period. When she did not get a birthday card from her father she went to the police because she believed that he was dead. San Diego elder abuse attorneys warn family members that any time they cannot get in touch with a senior family member that something may be seriously wrong.

The body of Gerald Rabourn has never been found. The caregiver has been charged with 11 counts. In addition to the murder with special circumstances, she was charged with elder abuse, embezzlement by a trustee, forgery, grand theft, and auto theft.

Caregiver accused of abusing residents at Phoenix assisted-living facility

The Arizona Republic-12 New Breaking News Team[17]
Fri Jan 17, 2014 7:36 PM
By Weslie Swift

An adult caregiver has been arrested in connection with attacks on residents at an assisted-living facility in north Phoenix.

According to court documents obtained Friday, two residents at Sunset Vista First, an assisted-living facility near Union Hills Drive and Second Avenue, said that Zaith Wilfredo Contreras, 33, had been "practicing his karate" on them.

Investigators say that Contreras left one resident who uses a wheelchair breathless after authorities say Contreras punched him in the center of his chest. The same resident reported that Contreras kicked him in the back, nearly ejecting him out of his chair.

---

[17] http://www.azcentral.com/community/surprise/articles/20140117caregiver-accused-abusing-residents-assisted-living-facility-surprise-abrk.html

Another resident told officials that Contreras held her throat while striking the canvas back of her wheelchair with his knee. As a result, she suffered a broken rib and bruising, court documents say.

Victims say that, during the abuse, Contreras would tell them, "You're making me do this," and "I'm doing this to make you a better human."

Authorities say that Contreras threatened both victims, telling them that if they reported the abuse, he would "hurt them so bad they would wish they had never talked."

According to court documents, Contreras became aware that he was being investigated when records were requested for the two victims and a third victim, who died of similar injuries in March. Detectives are continuing to investigate that case, court records say.

Contreras began working at the facility in July 2012; he quit his job in September when he learned of the investigation, court records say.

Investigators believe he was evading the police by living with various family members. When Contreras appeared in court on a DUI warrant on Monday, he was also taken into custody on suspicion of two counts of physical abuse on a vulnerable adult.

Contreras told police he could hurt someone because of his black belt in karate and experience as a mixed-martial-arts specialist, but he denied any abuse. Contreras then identified strike points on the body that cause injuries, records show. Investigators said the points Contreras demonstrated were the same spots where the victims reported being struck.

Feb 27, 2014 10:20 PM
by Stefanie Boe

Tucson - A Tucson man is accused of sexually assaulting a patient at an assisted living center where he worked as a CNA.

47-year old Kenneth Wilson was arrested Thursday. The investigation started back in December when the Tucson Police Department received information about a 79-year old woman being sexually assaulted and sexually abused at the Villa Maria Care Center, located in the 4300 Block of East Grant Rd.

The victim reported that the incidents took place on several different occasions throughout 2013 by a Certified Nursing Assistant who worked at the Center.

Police say the Villa Maria Care Center fully cooperated with detectives and agents during the investigation.

Wilson was booked into the Pima County Jail on two counts of Sexual Assault (F2), two counts of Sexual Abuse (F5) and one count of Emotional Abuse of a Vulnerable Adult (F6).

Wisconsin caregiver accused of breaking baby's leg[19]

January 28, 2014 6:30 am
The Leader-Telegram (Eau Claire)

Neillsville -- A Colby day care operator has been charged in Clark County Court with a felony count of child abuse for reportedly breaking the leg of

---

[18] http://www.kvoa.com/news/caregiver-accused-of-sexually-assaulting-patient/
[19] http://lacrossetribune.com/news/local/wisconsin-caregiver-accused-of-breaking-baby-s-leg/article_88a4d707-11d9-5c2c-8dcc-fbbc5f55ac56.html

a 7-month-old girl and then not telling the mother out of fear the mother would "flip out."

Kaylee A. Schnitzler also is charged with a misdemeanor count of child neglect. The felony has a maximum penalty of 10 years in prison. Her initial court date is Feb. 6.

According to court records:

A woman told police she has three children, including the 7-month-old, who attend Schnitzlerâs Dream Bound day care center. The mother picked up the children on Oct. 9 and was told by Schnitzler that the infant had been crying for about two hours.

At home, the infant continued to cry and had a swollen and "odd" positioned left leg. The girl was taken to a doctor, who said the child had a "displaced femur fracture." Another doctor said "a large amount of force is necessary to fracture a bone and that it was unlikely for a non-cruising infant to generate the force necessary to cause the fracture."   □ □

Schnitzler initially told police she was unaware of any injury to the child, saying the girl ate and slept as normal. In subsequent police interviews, she said she "adjusted" the girl's leg while holding her, so her leg was not bent. She said she did not pull on the leg hard and heard the girl's sleeper unsnap. She said the girl was not fussy.

Schnitzler later said she thought it was the girl's leg snapping and not the sleeper buttons, and that it was possible that she hurt the girl's leg at that time, around 11:30 a.m. She said she put the child in a play pen several times because she could not take the constant crying.

Schnitzler repeatedly told police she did not call the mother because she was afraid the mother would "flip out" or "freak out on her."

A nearly 4-year-old who was at the day care that day told police Schnitzler threw the infant on the floor.

BACKGROUND CHECKS – DO THEY REALLY WORK?
Chapter Three

Logic would suggest that utilizing a thorough background screening process would drastically curtail individuals with a propensity for abuse. While that is true, it is the system that is broke. The issues with background checks include the fact that they are not required in all settings, the manner of conducting backgrounds is not uniform, there is no national requirements and not all states require background searches be conducted. Most caregiver facilities rely upon the process of sending a background form into the state's law enforcement agency. This can take weeks or months for the response to be returned. Some use the various Department of Public Safety's public website that many states make available. According to a study of the Texas Department of Public Safety's public website, they failed as much as they succeeded:

Star Telegram[20]
Ft. Worth, TX.

Criminal background checks used to screen teacher applicants, doctors, nurses and daycare employees may not turn up their arrest records because of critical gaps in the Texas criminal records database, a new state audit shows.

Prosecutors and courts have *failed to submit* to the state disposition records on about *one of every four arrests in 2009*, the audit found. While that is a slight improvement from a 2006 audit, it still means that the Department of Public Safety Computerized Criminal History System is not a reliable source for complete information, the audit found.

State law requires courts and prosecutors to submit the information within 30 days of receiving it.

"It is important to note, however, that DPS cannot control whether prosecutor offices and courts submit all records because the Texas Code of Criminal

[20] http://www.star-telegram.com/2011/09/29/3406283/database-gaps-hinder-texas-criminal.html#ixzz1ZMlbdbBI

Procedure does not provide DPS with the ability to penalize prosecutor offices and courts for not submitting information," the audit states.

Auditors visited the Tarrant County District Attorney's office, as well as prosecutors' offices in Harris County to find out why records weren't being submitted. They pointed to some computer problems, saying they may not receive rejection or error notices when the DPS system does not accept records they submit. The county officials also said that they cannot submit some records because they lack required arrest incident numbers or state identification numbers. In Tarrant County, for example, 1,730 probation records lacked the state identification number.

The State Auditor's Office also said that DPS should improve the timeliness and accuracy of data in its Criminal History System.

For example, the report notes that *1,634 (7.65 percent) of 21,351 offenders* admitted to jail, prison, or probation by the Texas Department of Criminal Justice in November 2010 *did not have corresponding prosecutor and court records in the DPS system.* "In addition, information that DPS provides as part of its criminal history background checks does not include probation records," according to the report.

According to a study conducted in 2011 by the Office of Inspector General[21] **"Almost all nursing facilities employed one or more individuals with at least one criminal conviction.** Our analysis of FBI-maintained criminal history records revealed that

1) Ninety-two (92%) percent of nursing facilities employed at least one individual with at least one criminal conviction.

2) Nearly half of nursing facilities employed five or more individuals with at least one conviction.

3) Forty-four percent of employees with convictions were convicted of crimes against property (e.g., burglary, shoplifting, writing bad checks), making it the most common type of crime committed.

4) Overall, 5 percent of nursing facility employees had at least one conviction in FBI-maintained criminal history records.

5) Most convictions occurred prior to employment.

---

[21] Dept. of Health and Human Services · OEI-07-09-00110

6) Eighty-four percent of employees with convictions had their most recent conviction prior to their beginning date of employment.

Despite the lack of a Federal requirement for nursing facilities to conduct criminal background checks, most States required, and/or nursing facilities reported conducting, some type of background check. Forty-three States required nursing facilities to conduct either an FBI or a statewide criminal background check for prospective employees. Some nursing facilities located in the remaining eight States reported conducting criminal background checks even though they were not required to do so. All but 2 percent of nursing facilities reported conducting some type of background check".

The report was very insightful but brought forth distinctions made between facilities accepting federal funding and those that do not and continued by stating:

Nursing facilities participating in Medicare and Medicaid are required to provide services that maintain the dignity and well-being of all residents. Federal regulation prohibits Medicare and Medicaid nursing facilities from employing individuals found guilty of abusing, neglecting, or mistreating residents by a court of law. Employment of individuals who have had a finding entered into the State nurse aide registry concerning abuse, neglect, or mistreatment of residents or misappropriation of their property is also prohibited.

Neither Federal law nor regulation specifically requires that nursing facilities check State or Federal Bureau of Investigation (FBI) criminal history records for prospective employees. Despite this, nursing facilities have access to FBI criminal history records to conduct criminal background checks on individuals applying for positions involving direct patient care. Some States require such checks under their own authority.

Table 1: Nursing Facility Criminal Background Check Requirements by State

Type of Check Required	States	Number of States
FBI and Statewide	AK, AZ, DE, ID, MI, MS, NM, NV, NY, TN	10
Statewide*	AR, CA, DC, FL, GA, IL, IN, IA, KS, KY, LA, ME, MD, MA, MN, MO, NE, NH, NJ, NC, OH, OK, OR, PA, RI, SC, TX, UT, VA, VT, WA, WV, WI	33
None	AL, CO, CT, HI**, MT, ND, SD, WY	8
Total		51

The Federal Bureau of Investigation maintains the national criminal database (National Crime Information Center or NCIC) that law enforcement officials utilize to determine if a subject has a criminal history. Each state has a similar database. Unless the person is arrested by federal authorities where the level of criminal activity is extreme (drug cartel, distribution of narcotics, etc.), the majority of arrest records are housed in the District Court Clerk's office in each county. When an arrest is made, law enforcement officials submit the information to the District Attorney for prosecution. Therefore, the best source of information is at the County District Clerk level.

When a person is arrested, law enforcement officials are *supposed* to send a copy of the information to their state's Department of Public Safety so this information can be inserted into the state's database and be available for police within the state. They are also *supposed* to send the information to the FBI for inclusion in the NCIC database. As we see from the previously mentioned study, this is not done in 1 out of 4 cases.

Facilities chose to utilize their respective state's law enforcement system because (a) they are required to do so by law (b) they feel it is cheaper than using a professional background screening company or (c) this is the only method they are aware of due to this being a common practice within the industry.

The report from the Office of Inspector General[22] showed that the Federal records are incomplete just as those compiled by the State law enforcement agencies. "The criminal history record information we received from FBI

---

[22] Dept. of Health and Human Services - OEI-07-09-00110

suggested that the records did not contain all of the convictions for particular employees. For example, criminal history record information contained notations of probation violations (suggesting that a conviction occurred), but the record did not contain the convictions leading to the imposition of probation periods. In addition, many charges had no corresponding disposition information (e.g., conviction, dismissal), so we could not determine whether a conviction occurred. Finally, it is possible that some individuals' records did not contain convictions because they were removed following a judicial diversion program (e.g., completion of an alcohol and substance abuse education course)".

Percentage of Nursing Facilities That Employed Various Percentages of Employees With Criminal Convictions

Percentage of Employees With Criminal Convictions	Percentage of Nursing Facilities
None	7.7%
Up to 5.0%	51.8%
Greater than 5.0% to 10.0%	26.0%
Greater than 10.0% to 15.0%	6.3%
Greater than 15.0% to 20.0%	5.7%
Greater than 20.0% to 25.0%	2.5%
Total	100.0%

Categories of Crimes for Which Nursing Facility Employees Were Convicted

Category of Crime	Percentage of Employees With Criminal Convictions
Crimes against property	43.6%*
Other	26.4%
DUI	20.3%
Drug-related crimes	16.2%
Crimes against persons	13.1%
Driving-related crimes other than DUI	11.9%

Nursing Facility Employees With Certain Job Classifications Who Had Convictions

Job Classification	Percentage of Employees With Convictions
Housekeeping/laundry/maintenance/security	6.5%
Certified nursing and medication aides	6.4%
Dietary	5.7%
Nursing (e.g., registered and licensed practical nurses)	3.6%
All other	2.7%
Administration	2.6%

Facilities that truly want to provide more accurate background checks can utilize independent professional background companies. Caution should be used when selecting the right company as most states require the company to be licensed as a private investigation agency. Estimates indicate that approximately half of those companies providing background checks are not properly licensed to do so.

One of the things that make using an independent background screening company more reliable than the state is the methods utilized. Whereas law enforcement data is only information that *should have* been reported by the arresting agency, data from third-party vendors are much more complete. A background check through one of these sources can be adjusted for the individual client's needs but the majority of searches utilize the following sources of information:

- Department of Public Safety
- Department of Corrections
- Administration of the Court
- Office of Foreign Assets Control (OFAC) Nationals List
- General Services Watch List
- CIA Public Exposed List
- United Nations Sanctions List
- World Bank Ineligible List
- U.S. Federal Courts (Pacer)
- National Sex & Violent Offender Database

By checking the County's District Clerk record, the State's Department of Public Safety's records, the State's Department of Corrections (shows anyone having been incarcerated) as well as the other searches, you get a much broader search.

While the information available through a third-party background screening company is better information in totality, laws such as the Fair Credit Reporting Act (FCRA) have made handcuffed employers and background screening companies. The name, "Fair Credit" Reporting Act is misleading as the FCRA uses a very broad brush to dictate the responsibilities of both the employer and screening company related to the use of background checks. This act is very difficult to fully understand and many Human Resource Managers chose to air on the side of caution. For example, the FCRA states that *arrest records* can only be considered going back a period of 7 years. However, there is no limit on how far back *conviction records* can be provided. Some companies have a policy of only considering information going back 7 years, regardless of whether it is an arrest or a conviction.

It is ironic that if you want to investigate your neighbor, there are no restrictions on doing so but when considering a person for a position that could cause physical, financial or other devastating liability, there are great restrictions. I should qualify this statement because there are some searches that a person (or employer) cannot legally conduct without the specific authorization of the person. One would be obtaining a credit report on a person. A separate and distinct authorization must be obtained for this type of search.

The FCRA mandates that an employer must get written authorization to run a background check and that if any negative information is found, they must also provide them with a letter advising them of the adverse information. The candidate can ask for a re-investigation if they feel the information is not correct. There are groups and agencies like the EEOC who are trying to make it so that an employer cannot consider information if it doesn't directly apply to the position and duties of the job. For instance, if a person was charged with driving under the influence but is applying for a clerical position, this should not be considered according to their thinking. My contention is the person may advance within the company and drive a company vehicle or operate heavy machinery. This is just one of the examples of how employers are having their hands tied when trying to find the best qualified individual to hire.

Even with these limitations a third-party background screening company is more capable, faster and provides better information. Facilities who employ caregivers typically respond by saying they are following legislative procedures by submitting the backgrounds to the state. Few will undertake additional expense to have a background screening in lieu of or in conjunction with the state backgrounds.

A government agency cannot be sued, except under extreme circumstances. If I were an employer who hires caregivers, I would want to limit my liability by having a third-party private background screening company. Additionally, these outside agencies are faster than those by the state.

In a perfect world, background checks should dramatically reduce neglect and abuse. In the real world, background checks are just one of many tools required to stop the tide of abuse.

WHAT IS NURSING HOME ABUSE?
Chapter Four

To investigate nursing home abuse, you must first understand what "abuse" actually is, where it comes from and the characteristics associated with the abuse. According to the Funk and Wagnall's Standard Dictionary, abuse is "to use improperly or injuriously; to misuse, to hurt by treating wrongly; to injure or to speak in coarse or bad terms." When applied to nursing homes, it is to intentionally miss-handle or to verbally degrade a person. For the most part, the abuse is an intentional action or actions that have formed a pattern in which the person is treated. Let's face it; accidents happen to everyone in every type of job and situation. However, abuse is going beyond an "accident" and has a direct correlation to the mental frame of mind or condition of the person(s) involved.

By the time a person finds themselves in a nursing home, they have usually reached a sense of helplessness and are insecure about themselves and their future. Although this topic is not a laughing matter, I am often reminded of the elderly patient who indicated that they go to the bathroom regularly at 6:00 A.M. every morning. Unfortunately, they are not awake when they do! This is just an example of how the elderly become dependent on those around them in their later period of life. These people, for the most part, have worked a long life and only hope that they can leave this world with a little bit of respect and dignity. It is bad enough that they lose control of their bodily functions and motor skills, but being the victim of abuse is more than any these people deserve.

Abuse can come from a variety of causes, however, all abuse has the same characteristic of an intentional action. Regardless of the reason, a willful intent is a fundamental characteristic for the abuse to have occurred. Unfortunately, some people are unhappy with their own life and they take this out on everyone around them. The elderly are an easy target because they are weak and defenseless. In many cases, the patient has had a stroke or other medical condition that has caused them to lose their speech or their motor skills. When a person is unable to speak or to resist, the patient can often times become a target of the abuse.

SCOPE OF ABUSE AND NEGLECT[23]

1.4 million — Current number of people who are living in U.S. nursing homes.

20,673 — Complaints of abuse, gross neglect, and exploitation on behalf of nursing home and "board and care" residents in 2003.

1 in 14 — Number of incidents of elder abuse reported to authorities.

90% — Percentage of U.S. nursing homes with staffing levels too low to provide adequate care.

PROFIT MOTIVES AND CARE IN THE NURSING HOME INDUSTRY

$75 billion — State and federal financing of the nursing home industry in 2006.

$34 billion — Contribution of nursing home residents and their families in 2001.

$3.4 billion — Suspicious accounting transactions identified by U.S. News & World Report in 2000.

31% — Extent to which deficiencies in care in for-profit nursing homes was higher than in non-profit nursing homes in 2006.

16% — Drop in nurse assistants' hours per resident day.

There are many forms of abuse including verbal, emotional and physical. Some of the more commonly found types of abuse include:

- Verbally degrading the patient

---

[23] http://www.justice.org/cps/rde/justice/hs.xsl/3005.htm

- Verbally threatening the patient

- Emotionally manipulating the patient

- Emotionally threatening the patient

- Physically injuring the patient

- Physically manipulating the patient

- Sexually abusing the patient

Verbally Degrading the Patient:

This is one of the more common type of abuse found in nursing home facilities. It is common for the staff of a facility to yell and scream at other employees, as well as the patients in their care. When confronted with this, the staff usually falls back on the catch-all defense of "the person is hard of hearing." It is one thing to increase the volume of one's voice, but it is another thing to scream degrading remarks at the person. One of the more common ways that a patient is degraded verbally is when they are told that if they don't eat, the employee will shove the food down their throat. There are proper ways to tell a person what you want them to do and this is not one of them.

Many of the nursing home employees are kind to the patients and speak kindly when they clean them by telling them such things as, "you have such pretty hair." However, it is also common for the employee to tell them degrading remarks about their condition or their inability to control their bodily functions. The elderly are frightened and disoriented by being in a nursing home. Having someone speak rudely or harshly towards them causes the patient further discomfort. The elderly feel defenseless in these situations and are just happy to have someone who will pay a little attention to them, regardless of the abuse. The facility employee who carries on this activity knows that the elderly are threatened by them and are therefore not concerned with treating the person with respect and dignity. Every nursing home has employees who verbally abuse their patients and most over-look the employee's actions because they at least show up for work or they pass it off as the person having a bad day.

Verbally Threatening the Patient:

Verbally threats are very similar to verbal abuse in general; however, they tend to be directed much more towards a particular patient and it is more intense than normal verbal abuse. When an employee degrades a patient by telling them that they don't like the person wetting all over themselves while using a sarcastic voice that is verbally degrading. However, when an employee tells the patient that they are going to spank the person if they keep wetting the bed, this becomes a type of verbal threat. The patient does not have control of their bodily functions and can therefore not prevent or control this situation.

Emotionally Manipulating the Patient:

An elderly person who is insecure about their situation and condition is a prime candidate for emotional manipulation. An example of this comes to mind. The President of the United States decided to stop in a nursing home to conduct some public relations. One of the elderly patients carried on a conversation with him for a while and the President finally asked, "You don't know who I am, do you?" The patient said, "no, but if you will go to the nurse's station over there, they will tell you who you are." This is a simple way of depicting how a patient can become insecure about their surroundings.

The patient has the primal instinct to be around other people who they feel will protect and care for them. Facility employees know that a patient will often endure hardship just to have someone around them. People are born with the desire to be touched and communicated with. When the elderly do not have enough of this attention, they are easily manipulated. In some cases patients they can be emotionally maneuvered into over-looking the abuse of the staff in fear of not receiving the necessary attention that they crave.

Emotionally Threatening the Patient:

A patient is emotionally threatened when they have had certain circumstances occur that they perceive as a threat and which keeps them from speaking out against the threat. When a patient observes another patient being mistreated and no one does anything about it, they begin to become emotionally threatened into realizing that they have no control over their situation. They believe that they must therefore keep silent to prevent themselves from being a target. The patients are quick to observe the treatment of those around them and it doesn't take long to understand that they are emotionally at a disadvantage.

Physically Injuring the Patient:

There are many ways that a patient can be physically injured while in a nursing home. Dropping or mishandling a patient is fairly routine occurrences in most facilities. Although handling a person in certain ways may not be considered rough on a younger person, when applied to the elderly, it can definitely be abuse. The elderly have problems with brittle bones and are fragile to begin with. When an employee tosses a person onto the bed, it is not uncommon for the patient to dislocate their hip or break a bone.

Because the skin of an elderly person loses its elasticity, their skin can be torn and cut with the least amount of effort. Failing to take extra care while handling the person is once again is a way skin can be damaged.

Almost all nursing homes are understaffed, which prevents the patients from being routinely turned to prevent bed sores (pressure sores). This physically injures the patient and the pain has been described as being similar to an ulcer in a person's mouth but even worse. When a bed sore is left untreated, it turns into a sepsis (open wound) where infection occurs. These patients often are left unchecked and lay in their own urine which further irritates and contaminates the sepsis.

Another type of physical abuse is grabbing a patient by the checks and attempting to force-feed the subject. The patient may not like the food and most facilities try to provide a secondary meal for these situations. Unfortunately, the person may be abused by forcing them to eat and end up with cuts and abrasions.

Nursing home facilities are not created equal and do not have the same bathroom facilities. Some may have individual bathrooms and bathing facilities, however, for the most part the majority has only have 2-5 baths and/or showers. Because of the lack of bathing facilities, the patients may not receive proper cleaning, which is another type of physical abuse. The types and variety of abuses will be discussed later in this book.

Physically Manipulating the Patient:

A patient can be physically manipulated into performing or conducting certain actions that they would not customarily perform. As an example, the patient may be coerced into moving or standing against their will based on a firm grip or pinch by a staff member. These types of employees attempt to get the patient to move at a faster rate or in a manner that they feel appropriate by pinching or strongly grabbing the person. The goal is to cause the person to perform the desired activity without leaving a physical mark on the patient.

Sexually Abusing the Patient:

A patient that is mentally slow, physically unable to speak, or unable to defend themselves may become a victim of sexual abuse. These attacks may come from a staff member, another patient, a family member or a complete stranger. Even when it comes from a staff member, other employees are often too busy to notice unusual signs or they may neglect to report the incident out of fear. The nursing homes are typically co-ed and it is not uncommon for relationships to develop as it would in any male/female setting. However, when one patient sexually abuses another, this moves outside of a normal relationship just as it would in any other social setting.

Family members may miss the affection and relationship with their spouse who is a patient. When this occurs, they often attempt to continue their sexual relationship. Unfortunately, the medical conditions as well as physical, mental and emotional status of the relative may cause the intercourse to be painful. If this takes place against the will of the spouse, it moves into the area of sexual abuse. In some situations, the nursing home staff will not do anything about it based on the fear of reprisals due to the legal relationship between the couple.

In a nursing home setting, abuse can come from a variety of persons. This includes the owner(s) of the nursing home, the administrator of the nursing home, the staff of the facility and the family members. In addition, abuse can come from other patients (or residents as they are commonly called) or even someone off of the street. The State Licensing Board is usually a promoter of this activity due to their lack of inspections and enforcement. The following will attempt to describe how each of these can be involved in abuse of nursing homes:

Nursing Home Owner(s):

The owners of a nursing home can be a variety of people with a diverse background. They may be doctors, independent businessmen, large corporations or family owned operations. As in many industries, the nursing home industry is seeing many of the small homes being bought out and placed with a large conglomeration of other nursing homes under a central corporation. One can be as bad as the other. The smaller owners have less cash flow, while the larger corporations provide less personal contact. Unfortunately, all of the owners are forced to recognize that it is a business and they make decisions based on profit, which effects the treatment, staff and supplies available to the patients. Large corporations typically have stockholders which demand as much profit from the homes as possible. Because they are large, an impersonal approach often develops, making cutting services to increase profit even easier. This impersonal attitude permeates into a lack of control. The lack of control allows administrators to carry on without proper supervision. The lack of supervision transfers into a lack of patient care, which turns into abuse.

The owners of nursing homes are known for hiring minimum wage employees who typically have minimal education. Even the Licensed Vocational Nurses (LVN) and the Registered Nurses (RN) that work at the nursing homes are often sub-standard when compared to other LVN's or RN's employed in hospitals. You also see nurses moon-lighting to pick-up extra pay by working their off-hours at nursing homes. Because the owners can hire employees to do the job at a minimum pay level, they continue to do so. In reality, if they would increase the rate of pay, the quality of employees would increase which would ultimately translate into better care, more profits and less lawsuits.

The owners of these facilities seldom, if ever, conduct any type of background investigations on the potential employee. During our investigations, we have found that many of the employees go from one nursing home to the next. When someone is terminated for abuse or something similar, they simply move on to the next nursing home that is more than willing to hire someone already "trained" in the industry. Failing to conduct appropriate background checks has resulted in the industry cultivating an atmosphere of abuse. We have seen situations where an administrator becomes known for hiring those who have had conflicts with the law and these people flock to the administrator who is more than willing to hire them.

The bottom line with the majority of nursing home owners is the profit margin. They lose sight of the care and become too concerned with making a profit and end up promoting the problems which are ruining the industry.

The Nursing Home Administration:

The administrators at a nursing home facility ultimately determine the care or abuse that the patients obtain. If they allow abuse, neglect and poor care to occur, they are in essence promoting this type of treatment. Often, the administrators intentionally try to shield themselves from the rest of the staff so they can state that they did not know that a situation was occurring. Most administrators are known for staying in their office and seldom walking the hallways to see what is actually going on. These same administrators tell the supervisors who advise them of a situation that they "will take care of it" and then never take any action. After this occurs over and over again, the supervisors stop telling the administrators because they know nothing will be done. This is exactly what the administrators want because they can once again blame the supervisors and cry that they never knew about the abuse.

The administrators fail to order supplies in an effort to please the owners by keeping supply costs down. There are times where the administrators told employees to stop wearing gloves when working with patients because they were costing too much. During investigations, supplies are found to be limited until just before the State Auditors come in to perform an audit. They usually have a closet with new sheets, towels, linens, etc… stocked and will take these out just while the auditors are there and then will take the supplies away afterwards.

The administrators will often order their employees to fill-in the blank spaces on charts so that it will not stick out when the State Auditors arrive. This attitude then tells the staff that they can cheat or break other laws since the administration is encouraging this activity.

Investigations have typically shown that the administrators of a facility often are caught in the middle. They are being pressured by the owners to produce profits while the staff treats them like an enemy as well. The stress from both sides causes the administrator to hide in their office away from both sides.

The Nursing Home Staff:

The employees of the nursing home are the ones who ultimately have the most contact with the patients and are therefore the ones who are most likely to abuse the patients. Their actions, however, are allowed and cultivated by the actions of the facility owners and the administrators. Employees have confided that the employees do the things they do because they observed the Director of Nurses or the Charge Nurse engaging in the activity.

The employees are minimum wage earners who typically have a poor self-esteem and take life's frustrations out on those who can't defend themselves. In all fairness, these employees are over-worked and there is a shortage of staff which causes their tolerance level to decrease. Some of the patients can become a little violent when they are ill or tired and the staff has to guard against patients who will vent this towards the staff. However, if trained properly, they should know how to deal with this issue.

Family Abuse:

Although abuse by family members is very rare, it does happen. In one case, a lady was a patient in the nursing home and her husband would come in and have intercourse with her. The patient had a Foley tube and the employees would hear her moaning and crying due to the intercourse causing her pain. Although the staff heard and knew, no one tried to stop this from occurring. In abuse by family members, the abuse usually escalates into some type of physical violence which was a result of a continued problem between the two. This is even less likely to occur due to there being so many employees in and out of the rooms. Even though this is very rare, this issue should still be considered based on the merits of the investigation.

Abuse by Other Residents:

One patient abusing another patient occurs from time to time and needs to be addressed as a possibility. When a patient has had a stroke or other medical condition that prohibits them from speaking and/or moving, they can become a target of abuse. Patients can steal from these subjects, pinch, hit or sexually abuse this type of resident. There are cases where a patient sneaks around sexually abusing patients who were not mentally coherent.

Abuse by Strangers:

Many nursing homes lack up-to-date security and in some of the facilities located in crime-ridden areas, they become a target. When you have transients in the area, they will often try to sneak into the homes to use the bathroom and showers or to get out of the heat and cold. Although their original intent may have been somewhat harmless, crimes occur due an opportunity presenting itself.

Most nursing homes have doors located on all four sides of the structure which are not observed on a regular basis. The homes generally have policies indicating that all of the doors except the front door have to be locked after a certain period of time. However, employees use these doors to step outside to smoke and do not concern themselves with the security of the doors.

Domestic violence has been documented as carrying over into the facility and a lack of security in these facilities is fails to discourage this activity.

Promotion of Abuse by the State Board:

The State Health Board or a similar licensing board regulates the nursing home facilities. Part of their job is to inspect and audit the facilities using surprise visits. It is a common occurrence for the nursing homes to know in advance that an audit was coming. Having fore-knowledge allows the administrators to pull out the new linen and supplies that they never use. In addition, this allows the administrators to cover their tracks by filling in charts, adding times sheets to make it appear that there are more employees and similar set-ups. This type of activity promotes the entire abuse situation.

As you can see, abuse stems from a variety of persons and may not be just the physical attack of a person. Failing to provide for the care and custody of a patient who is in the nursing home's care can move into the area of abuse. The emotional, physical and mental capabilities of each person involved can play a role in determining whether the action, or lack of action, is actually abuse. In addition, the intentions of the parties involved also have an effect on whether abuse has occurred or not. Most laws are written whereby the prosecution must prove it was the intent of the person to abuse another. It is often hard to prove the mindset and thinking of the person who committed the abuse.

THE DIFFERENCE BETWEEN
ABUSE AND NEGLECT
Chapter Five

There is a fine line between abuse and neglect. Sometimes neglect can become excessive and reach the point of abuse. When we think of abuse, we think of someone hitting or physically abusing a person. Abuse is commonly an intentional act that causes harm and empowers another. Neglect may be an intentional or an unintentional act and may be based on several factors such as the amount of employees on duty or the laziness of the employee. In simple terms, neglect is failing to meet the needs of the patient.

A common epidemic among facilities is under-staffing and the employees are usually being poorly trained. Even when a person has a good attitude about their job and they have a genuine desire to complete the tasks in the described manner, it may be impossible for them to do so if they are short-staffed and have too many patients to care for. Many times, one aide will be responsible for 6-60 patients by themselves. Unless the patients are strictly bed-ridden, 6-10 patients per aid is an acceptable ratio in the industry. However, when one aide is called upon to provide care for more than this, it is obvious that even the best efforts can simply not fulfill the needs of this many patients. When a patient is forced to lie in their own urine for extended periods of times because the aide is off helping someone else, this is neglect. Sometimes an aide is asked to assist another employee in moving, lifting or changing a patient. This takes the aide from the needs of the patients they have been assigned.

In all professions, there are some people who are simply lazy and who do not want to work. This seems to be prevalent in the nursing home industry. It is common to find the aides in a patient's room with the curtain drawn, concealing the fact that they are watching television. Employees sleeping on duty are another regular occurrence. Anyone who has ever worked in a nursing home facility will tell you that there is always too much work to watch T.V. or to take a nap. When this occurs, a patient is not being checked properly and neglect then occurs.

There are those facilities that simply do not have the physical capabilities to take care of the number of patients that they are handling. Often the home was built to accommodate one person to a room and it has changed to two people per room. This takes a toll on all things because the kitchen was designed to feed less people, the nurse's desk was designed for fewer nurses, the bathrooms were made for less people and these things aide in the neglect of the patients.

Older nursing home facilities also tend to have older pieces of equipment that breaks down or has not been replaced at all. The failure of equipment to monitor a patient or to operate properly poses another type of possible neglect. Although the staff may not intentionally try to neglect the patient, if the equipment isn't working when the patient needs the equipment, the resident is neglected.

Another form of neglect is simple verbal communication. Every person needs interaction with other humans, especially when they are scared and insecure about their life. Because the staff at nursing homes are always understaffed and are rushing around trying to complete the tasks that have to be done, they often fail to take time to engage in simple conversation with the patients. Elderly patients just want to hear another person's voice and to have someone act like they care about them. Unfortunately, this lack of verbal contact is another source of neglect that the patients must endure. In addition, some family members live out of town and are unable to visit their family regularly. This tends to magnify the lack of daily contact that the person fails to get from the staff members. In a lot of nursing homes, the patient does not have a telephone in their room and family members are even less available to contact the resident. Once again, the lack of contact further complicates the neglect factor in the life of the person.

Many patients are placed in a wheelchair in the morning at the beginning of a shift and are pushed to an area near a door or window where they congregate with other patients so they can look outside. In too many instances, the patients are left in the wheelchair until it's time for bed. This causes pressure sores to occur on the buttock area which is physical abuse. However, the person endures neglect as they are allowed to remain in this position without having someone check on them.

Nourishment or the lack thereof is a major problem in nursing homes. Due to the patient's physical condition, many of the patients require hand-feeding by the nursing home staff. When there is a lack of staff to fulfill this duty, the person is neglected and may not get to eat or may have to wait their turn, resulting in their food being cold. Food in these types of facilities is prepared with a lack of salt or other enhancements due to medical conditions and restrictions. The food is bland to begin with and patients will often need encouragement to eat. Allowing their food to get cold due to not having enough staff to feed the patients is a source of neglect and concern.

Neglect often occurs in a facility when a person needs assistance in getting out of bed and walking to the bathroom. Everyone wants to maintain their self-sufficiency by doing these types of tasks for themselves. However, many of the elderly reach the point where they know that they need assistance to do this and will ring the call button to get an aide to assist them in this endeavor. Because many of the staff members are often busy helping others, or they may simply be lazy, the call button goes unanswered for a period of time. When this occurs, the patient either lays in bed where they urinate and lay in this, or they are forced to try to make it to the bathroom by themselves. If they lay in their own urine, it is obviously uncomfortable and can cause infection in a bed sore. When they try to make it to the bathroom themselves, many of the patients fall and hurt themselves or even break bones.

Most of the patients in a nursing facility are required to take medicine and supplements on a regular basis and on a regular schedule. Once again, when the staff is short or you have aides that are allowed to be lazy, the person will not get these medications as directed by the doctor and further neglect occurs.

The basic premise to neglect is that a person in the care of the nursing home fails to receive the necessary treatment or care that they deserve. One of the types of neglect, in its self and by itself may not be extremely bad. However, it is not uncommon for most of these types of neglect to be occurring at the same time and over an extended period of time. The culmination of these activities causes physical and emotional scarring on the patient and is not the last things that a person should remember about life on this earth. As you can see from the preceding, neglect can take a variety of avenues and is often justified by the idea of lack of staffing. In fact, this is an excuse for an improperly ran facility which self- promotes neglect in their patients.

WHY NURSING HOMES ARE GETTING SUED
Chapter Six

The nursing home industry has failed to self-police their own profession and the state agencies that regulate the homes have failed as well. This lack of self-policing is causing families to come forward in increasing numbers to file lawsuits against the nursing home facilities. Large jury awards are being handed out in these cases because the jury members all have parents who may have been subjected to this type of inhumane treatment and they can identify with the victims and their families.

Nursing home abuses are becoming more widely discovered because some of the employees of these facilities are unsung heroes who step forward to tell the truth for what it is. The "whistle-blowers" law has aided in these individuals coming forward because the facilities cannot legally retaliate against an employee who "blows the whistle" on their employer. Investigations have documented that many of these employees have worked at all of the nursing homes in the area because they keep trying to find one that isn't as bad as the one they just left. After seeing the neglect and abuse at a nursing home, their conscious can't take it any longer and they decide to move on to another facility.

Unfortunately, this is an industry-wide problem that stems from the owners of nursing homes trying to drain every penny of profit out of the operation. When this occurs, the focus changes from how good of care they can give to the patient to simply keeping the home running without any major problems. In their quest for profit, the owners pay their staff slightly above minimum wages and the LVN's and RN's receive a lower pay than their counter-parts at hospitals. Obviously, if these people are getting paid less than others in the same field, they will eventually develop poor attitudes and moral will be low. Instead of paying a higher wage and getting a better trained and qualified employee to begin with, the industry keeps on with the poor standards. People need jobs, and because they need jobs, the nursing homes will always get employees who will work for the pay they provide. That doesn't make it right.

Hopefully one day the nursing home industry will realize that they are starting to pay more for lawsuits and bad publicity and will understand a simple principal of business. If they would simply pay their employees better, they would attract a better quality of person who is better trained.

If they can hire a better trained person who is making a pay level more in line with their counter-parts, their moral will be better, work will get done, the patients will be better treated and the nursing homes will not get sued. It simply comes down to the fact that they can pay more money up front or pay a lot more money when they are sued. None of the facilities seem to have caught on to this simple fact.

The general public is getting smarter and more concerned about this type of abuse and is starting to place hidden video cameras in their family's rooms to catch the abuse. However, because of privacy issues placing cameras in a room may be illegal. For example, Texas enacted a law in 2013 (Senate Bill 33) that amended the Health and Safety Code[24]. According to Section 555.025, you can only place a recording device in a room after getting authorization from the nursing home management. The actual wording is, "*Authorized* electronic monitoring" is "the placement of an electronic monitoring device in a resident's room and making tapes or recordings with the device *after making a request to the center to allow electronic monitoring*". The act goes on to spell out the civil and criminal penalties for violating this amendment. Obviously your likelihood of catching any activity on camera after getting permission to place a camera in the room is highly unlikely.

As the public gets better educated, there will be more eyes paying attention which will in turn create more opportunities for lawsuits.
Almost everyone has heard about "lawsuit abuse," and I don't think anyone is jumping for joy by the thought of more lawsuits, but this is the remedy set aside for seeking relief for neglect and abuse. The way to stop the lawsuits is to simply stop the abuse. The way to stop the abuse is for the nursing home industry to truly police themselves.

No one likes the idea of having their mother or father treated in this fashion, and I can assure you that this is going to be more concern as the "baby-boomer" generation gets older and we have more elderly that are going to have to be dealt with. The nursing home industry actually has the opportunity to make a great deal more money in the near future because of this. However, people will begin to take relatives into their own homes more or find some other manner in which to make their parent's last days more respectable and comfortable if the industry continues on their current course.

---

[24] www.capitol.state.tx.us/BillLookup/History.aspx?LegSess=83R&Bill=SB33

The State agencies that regulate the facilities are just as much to blame for this dilemma as anyone. Their job is to properly license and police the facilities. Of course, the first thing you hear from them is that they don't have enough staff or money and they are doing everything they can. Unfortunately, neither is true. For the most part, all government agencies have more money than they need because the government's solution to any problem is to throw more money at it. Nursing homes know ahead of time of upcoming inspections, allowing them time to fill in charts, put out new linen that is just there until the State leaves and reschedule employees so that there appears to be more on duty when the State is there than normal shifts. In essence, it is like a child getting told that the parents are coming upstairs to inspect their room in an hour and giving them enough time to push things under the bed and hide things out of sight.

There is going to have to be a more aggressive approach to regulating the industry, not more laws. There are plenty of laws, rules and restrictions. What is needed is someone who has enough desire and will-power to actually make truly unannounced inspections and hand out fines that will get the attention of the administrators. Some of the ways to over-come poor inspection habits are as follows:

✓ Make inspections more than once a year

✓ Make the inspections at a time that does not coincide with the renewal of a facility's license. They all know they have an inspection coming right before they are re-licensed.

✓ Create inspection "teams" consisting of more than one inspector. Even when the inspector arrives, word spreads through the home that an inspector is there and the other end of the facility has time to get their act together before the inspector can make it all the way to them. By sending at least two inspectors, one can start at one end and one at the other and cover more ground.

✓ Stiff fines need to be assessed for violations. The nursing home administrators understand money and that will get their attention.

✓ Post the inspections grades on the State's Internet site for the world to see. By doing this, you create bad publicity for those messing up and creates an incentive to change.

✓ Make sure that the inspectors have not worked at the nursing homes that they are inspecting as they form friendships that will not be broken. Many of the State inspectors worked in nursing homes before they went to work for the State and they still have contacts there.

✓ Increase the number of inspectors to a workable ratio between homes and inspectors

✓ Set guidelines for the inspectors requiring a certain number of inspections per week.

✓ Enact ordinances allowing nursing home records to be made available to public under the open records act.

✓ Require the financial statements of the nursing home facilities to be made public since public funds often pay for the patients and their treatment.

By enacting some or all of these suggestions, the industry will begin to see an improvement. Failing to do so will keep the facilities operating in a "business as usual" status which clearly is not working.

CASE EXAMPLES OF ABUSE
Chapter Seven

Through documented investigations that I have conducted relating to nursing homes, many things have been found to be common in each facility. The people and their attitudes are the same, their methods of abuse and neglect are the same and their ways of trying to cover it up is the same. We will discuss these more in-depth, however the following are examples of the things we have found in these investigations and are based on actual cases:

❑ In one case, an elderly lady was a resident of a nursing home for almost eight years. She was then moved to another home where she resided for almost two years before she passed away. Our agency was brought into the case because the lady passed away due to malnutrition and severe infections resulting from untreated bed sores. During the investigation, it was discovered that a male resident in the first nursing home had sexually abused our client. After she was moved to the new nursing home, she was handled improperly and was dropped causing her leg to break. The staff put a make-shift splint on the leg and never took her to the hospital. One of the aides stated that she later had to get on to a new aide because she was turning the client too roughly and her broken leg was not being supported when they turned her which caused more agony.

❑ In a separate case that we investigated, information revealed a nurse had taken a pillow and suffocated a patient. The death was never investigated and the nurse was terminated two weeks later for being intoxicated on the job.

❑ Our agency was asked to look into a nursing home after the client passed away. The reason for death on the death certificate was listed as "malnutrition." We found that the charts reflected the client was getting fed properly and that she was in fact eating very well. After a closer examination of the documents, it was found that the charts showed that she was being fed for four days after she had been admitted to the hospital and for six days after she passed away.

- In another case, the official record indicated the client died from complications from bed sore infections. Once again, the charts reflected that she was getting bathed, turned and treated regularly. When a closer examination of the charts was made, it was found that the employee who initialed the charts were not even on duty on the days the patient supposedly received all of these treatments.

- A client in one case passed away due to malnutrition. The charts reflected that the staff weighed the patient regularly. The charts once again told the truth. One week she records indicated the patient weighed 90 lbs. while the next she weighed 70 lbs. The numbers kept bouncing around in a dramatic fashion which is typically not possible for the body to endure. It would also have attracted attention and the doctor would have been called. Upon further investigation, numerous employee statements documented that they seldom, if ever, actually weighed the patients and simply guessed at the person's weight.

- In yet another case, a female patient had her husband come into her room occasionally and push the roommate into the hall. The female was very fragile and had several tubes coming out of her body for medical purposes. The husband would then have sexual intercourse with his wife and the staff testified that she could be heard screaming, moaning and crying because of the pain but the staff was told to not intervene.

- While investigating one nursing home facility, it was learned that the owner of the home was described as an alcoholic who had been shot in the stomach at a bar. His brother was described as a drug addict who was on the payroll but who was never seen. Their sister was the record administrator and was alleged to have had at least three nervous breakdowns.

- During the investigation of a facility, the employees indicated that the head RN would give other people's medicine to other patients to "knock them out" so she didn't have to put up with them.

- In the process of checking one facility out, it was determined that they had an aide who regularly spanked and pinched the patients who gave her any trouble.

- There was a nursing home facility that had several employees who were found to sneak out to their car at night and drink some alcohol before returning back to work.

- It was discovered in one case that a male patient was working in the laundry doing the laundry of other patients as well as the laundry of the nursing home.

- While checking on a client who had passed away due to malnutrition, we found that many of the staff members were eating the food that was supposed to go to the patients.

- During an investigation into a client who had fell trying to get out of bed and who was supposed to be bed ridden, it was determined that the staff moved the call light buttons away from the patients on a regular basis so they wouldn't bother the staff. The patient injured herself trying to make it to the bathroom.

- An investigation into a separate facility, it was determined that a patient had broken her hip. Upon a closer look we learned that a staff member "slam dunked" the patient into bed by throwing her out of the wheelchair and into the bed.

- It came to our attention in several cases that someone other than the licensed nurses and the medication aides were allowed to dispense medicine to patients.

- In yet another case, we determined that a nurse had given an aide some medicine to calm her nerves after she came to work upset over a family problem. The aide over-dosed on the medication and had to be rushed to the hospital.

- In the course of one investigation, it was discovered that the doors on the nursing home were never secured and a patient had recently wondered away from the home and was found a week later dead. The body was found out in the open in the field behind the nursing home.

- Our agency was asked to check on possible abuse that had occurred at a nursing home and we found that the staff often used physical restraints to tie the patients to the bed or wheelchair without a doctor's order simply to keep from dealing with the patient. It was also determined that the restraints were not checked on a regular basis as is required.

As you can see, the types of abuse run a wide array of courses. Many of these happen on a regular basis and as well as the more gruesome of abuse and neglect. While not as appalling on the surface, the following is a list of neglect and abuse that we have found in the majority of homes we have investigated:

- The staff in nursing homes tend to steal from the patients because everyone will blame it on the fact that they are old and senile and don't really know if they had the item or not.

- The patients are not turned or checked on a regular two hour interval as policies dictate. Failure to turn the patient creates pressure sores which turn into severe infections if not treated.

- The families who try to tend to their family members in the homes by bringing them special food and clothes usually end up having the food taken by the employees and the clothes used by other patients.

- The patients are placed in their wheelchairs early in the mornings and left there all day without being checked.

- The staff fails to check on the patients regularly, allowing them to lay in their own urine and body fluids.

- The dressing on wounds are not changed on a regular basis as noted by employees who initial the dressings and come in on their next shift to find the same dressings and initials.

- The patients are denied the opportunity to call family members even though it is not long distance.

- The call light buttons are ignored and/or moved away from the patient by the staff members.

- The staff members are often found taking naps in the patient's rooms.

- Many employees are found watching TV in patient's rooms.

- Staff members are known to smoke throughout the nursing home even though it causes respiratory problems for the patients who already have problems breathing.

- Many staff members are known to speak abusively towards the patients, including yelling and cursing.

- The staff members, on a regular basis, fail to properly document the in-put and out-put (drinking and urinating) of the patients.

- Many facilities are known to weight the patients only when they arrive at the home and then guess at their weight from that time on.

- The staff of nursing homes estimates the amount of food intake that a patient eats. It is found that most homes encourage the staff to over-state the amount of food the person eats.

- It is found that although the homes are supposed to have a supplement (such as Insure) or a secondary meal for the patient to eat if they don't like what is served, they seldom make this available to the patients.

- The homes are sometimes found to have two patients sharing a room which is supposed to be private and occupied by only one person.

- It is found that when a person dies, the doctors are called and often times the doctor tell the staff to log down the time of death. He will then sign the documents the next time he comes by, even though legally, a doctor is supposed to pronounce the person dead.

- In many homes, the staff does not have sufficient supplies, which includes gloves. The lack of gloves is responsible for the spread of bacteria and germs throughout the nursing home.

- It is found that in most homes, scarves (a skin fungus) is often spread throughout the home because the home will not quarantine the person who is infected.

- During the investigations, it has been determined that most homes use uncertified aides past the mandatory licensing period.

- The homes are found to have minimal orientation briefings for the staff and do not train them properly on the handling of the patients.

- Because of a shortage of staff, most aides have to turn and move patients without assistance, causing the patients to be handled too roughly or even dropped.

You can see that there are all kinds of ways that the records, treatment and care of the patients can be conducted incorrectly and manipulated. In addition, this also makes for easier cover-ups because the records are incorrectly kept to begin with.

HOW TO APPROACH THE INVESTIGATION
Chapter Eight

When conducting an investigation related to caregivers they are similar to other investigations that require your skills in interviewing; locating witnesses and record searches. Most often a P.I. will either get hired by the attorney who is representing someone abused in a nursing home or by the family themselves who may suspect that abuse is occurring. If the attorney hires you, the attorney may have already done some of your initial background and information gathering. When the family hires you, the investigator has to start from the ground up. You have to set the stage with the clients so they fully understand your involvement and how you can help. Because this may be a stressful and emotional period for them, they may ask you to do things that are unethical or illegal. They are hurt, frustrated and feel betrayed. Even so, it is your job to stay within the legal framework and coach the client appropriately. Your approach will help establish the success of the operation going forward.

Many times the family of a patient may not have any real indication that abuse is occurring but is highly suspicious. Due to the increase in media exposure, some family members simply want this possibility to be checked out to ease their own minds. However, the family may have observed some behavior or some bruises that lead them to the conclusion of abuse. The patient may have changed their behavior, became more withdrawn or shows alarm when a particular employee enters the room.

When dealing with family members, it is always best to remember that this is their relative and emotions may run high. It is a good habit to always question your clients and prepare them for the worse. People react differently and there are situations where family members become enraged to the point of violence when they discover the truth. Therefore, it is recommended that you spend time explaining the process of the investigation. Although attorneys work with P.I.'s on a regular basis, most individuals do not understand the way an investigator works. It will be to your benefit in the future if you take a little extra time during the initial interview and go through the process to prevent miss-communications in the future.

The P.I. should explain the steps that the investigator will take during the course of the investigation. While discussing this, the P.I. will get a better feel for the client's tolerance level. Ask the subject what their intentions are if you obtain information or actual video of the family member being miss-treated. Often, the person has never taken the thought process to its local conclusion in their mind. By causing them to think about this issue up front, they will not be as shocked later and will already have had time to deal with the whole situation. If the family does not have an attorney, you should suggest that they consult one before you even begin the investigation. In any situation such as this, it is always better to be working through the client's attorney whenever possible as the investigation then becomes a part of the attorney's "work product" which provides a better base for confidentiality. In addition, the attorney may suggest certain guidelines that they think will help the case.

Once you have established the proper communication with the family members, your course of investigation has to be determined. This is based on several factors such as the evidence that the family may have and whether the family member is still a resident of the facility. If the person is still residing within the facility, you may be able to explore the possibility of setting up hidden cameras to actually observe the treatment given the patient **(see information on page 56 related to legalities of using cameras).** Once again, it would be best to consult with the family's attorney as you may get into some legal issues.

When using hidden cameras, it is suggested that you use the kind without audio. Interception of audio is still a very vague area of the law and there are many cases regarding this issue, which are awaiting trial, which will soon dictate the course of this topic. However, until it is more clearly defined, it is suggested that audio be left out. After all, "a picture is worth a thousand words" and obtaining video of a person being mistreated will surely weigh heavily on the minds of a jury.

Another issue to deal with is the trespass laws and privacy issues. If the patient is in a totally private room, privacy issues may not be a problem. However, if the patient is sharing the room with another person, the privacy of the second person may become an issue. For the protection of the P.I., it is best that the family members involved sign a contract and hold-harmless clause. Hopefully your client will be able to tell you a lot about the other person in the room. If they are close with the family of the other patient and feel certain that they will not divulge their use of an investigator, it is suggested that they be contacted and get them to sign a hold-harmless clause as well. By doing this, the families are acknowledging that the cameras will be utilized and that they give permission for the cameras to be used. An important issue of this is remembering that there are usually one or two family members that have been given the patient's "power of attorney." These are the members of the family that should sign the contracts and hold-harmless agreements as they have the legal right to speak on behalf of the patient.

Once the legal issues surrounding utilizing hidden video cameras have been dealt with, you are then ready to put this into practice. There are many ways in which you can accomplish this. Some of these depend on the nature of the facility itself. You can get all types of pre-manufactured devices that already have a hidden camera in it. You may have to first check to see if the facility has a policy against brining in certain electrical items from the outside (regardless of them having a camera). You can always bring in a picture or wall clock that has a hidden camera in it. If all else fails, you can use chipboard video cameras and put them anywhere you need them. Most cameras now record to S.D. cards that you remove and place in a computer to review. Some may be hard-wired to go to a special long-play video recorder that will record from 12-48 hours, depending on which one you select. Another issue dealing with cameras is the use of more than one. With technology progressing, there is I.P. (internet cameras) that can be viewed over the internet. This requires access to an internet connection or Wi-Fi. Using the facilities is not wise as someone may recognize the device(s) using an unusual amount of bandwidth.

When anticipating the use of cameras, it is suggested that the family arrange to take you into the nursing home to see the actual set-up and the room in which the cameras will be used. Hopefully, the room will have the drop-down ceiling panels and some of the cameras and can be hidden up there. When placing the equipment, you should also consider accessibility. If you intend to leave the cameras in place for an extended period of time, you will have to be able to change out the S.D. cards and possibly batteries if not plugged into an electrical source. There are limited places in a nursing home room where you can put something that does not fit into the atmosphere. A liability of the human race is that most people seldom look up. For this reason, always remember that if you can put the camera and or recorders above eye levels, the chances that they will be discovered will be dramatically reduced.

When an attorney hires a P.I., it is usually after the fact and your job is to help prove what already has occurred. In many of these situations, the patient has already passed away. The attorneys that I have done for these cases for usually already have done some of the preliminary groundwork conducted. However, if they haven't you will have to start from scratch as you would when an individual hires you. For more information on the actual investigation techniques, please refer to the chapter on "how to conduct the investigation."

Ultimately the investigator has a responsibility to properly explain their involvement in the investigation, the realistic expectations and how the process works.

HOW TO CONDUCT THE INVESTIGATION
Chapter Nine

Regardless of whether you are hired by the family or the attorney, you will have to start by identifying possible witnesses. When an attorney hires you, some of this may have already been conducted. However, let's assume that you have to start from scratch. The investigation should concentrate on the following information:

❖ Police department records

❖ Court records

❖ State licensing records

❖ Doctor's records

❖ Hospital records

❖ Medical Examiner's records

You should first send a letter to the State Agency that regulates the nursing home industry in your particular State. Recite the Open Records Act in your request and ask for the following records:

➢ A list of employees who worked at the nursing home just prior to, during and shortly after the patient was at the facility.

➢ Request the social security numbers of the employees, their last known address and their date of birth. If you specify that you would like a copy of their licensing application, the information should be included on these.

➢ Ask for all records pertaining to any disciplinary action taken against the nursing home or any of the staff members during the time frame in question.

➢ Request a copy of the State's inspection records for the facility during the specified time frame.

➤ Ask for a copy of the facility's licensing records including the application, ownership and corporate records.

It should be noted that once you obtain these records you need to find out if any of the subjects are still employed at the facility. If they are, you should not interview the individual as this could pose a legal problem. Typically an investigator cannot do anything that would consider interfering with the operation of the business. If working for an attorney, they should advise you on this matter.

The State may try to avoid providing this information to you and may even ask for the State's Attorney General to rule on whether or not they have to release the information. In general, they will eventually have to release at least part of this information. If you are working for an attorney, they can usually get the information from the facility's attorney under a request for work product. Once you receive the information, you then need to verify the addresses of the employees. You will have a tremendous list of employees and initially you may not want to spend a great deal of time locating those subjects not readily located. Concentrate on those easily found until you run through this list.

The records should be closely scrutinized for information that may suggest certain employees who have had conflicts with the facility and who may therefore be adverse towards the nursing home. These are the employees that you should seek out first because they may have the most to say against the facility.

If you are working for an attorney, they will have already obtained copies of the patient's medical files and charts. When you are working for the family, ask them to request the information from the facility and include a request for the patient's daily charts which reflect their in-put, out-put, eating habits, medicines, etc... Regardless of which method you have to use to obtain the records, get them! After doing so, you should then ask for a list of employees and their schedules that worked during the time frame in question.

Once you have these, you can begin to check the charts. I can almost assure you that you will find the initials of employees on the chart who were not even working during the time frame in which they supposedly signed the charts. This is typical of when the nursing home gets in a hurry to make sure that there are no blank spaces on the charts that will draw the attention of the State inspectors. Remember, in all cases we have investigated, the facilities knew in advance that an inspection was coming. Some of the employees attempted to write in the initials of others on their shift that may have regularly been the person to have signed the charts. Fortunately, they seldom crosscheck the records to see if the person was actually working on the day in which they insert the initials.

If the client was taken to the hospital just before the patient died, check the charts because it is common to find where the employees inserted initials in the blanks of the charts even when the person wasn't even at the home. It is common to find the charts reflect that they were changing, feeding and taking care of the patient after the person had passed away. This shows several issues such as poor record keeping, intentional falsifying of records, poor management, an intentional cover-up of the nursing home's mistakes and inappropriate treatment of the patient (just to name a few).

The "drug charts" should be checked to see if the medications were being given to the patient on a regular basis. The patient's doctor should be contacted and a copy of their records obtained as well. These records should be matched against the orders in the nursing home records to insure that they reflect that the nursing staff properly received, executed and documented the orders by the doctor. The medicine should be checked to make sure that the doctor actually prescribed those that the facilities were giving to the patient. A check of the charts should be conducted to make sure that the person giving the medicine was licensed to do so. In addition, the records need to confirm that the person signing the drug chart was actually on duty on that particular date.

The daily charts of the patient should also be examined to see if there is an unusual change in the weight and eating habits of the patient. If the charts reflect that the subject's weight changed dramatically, it probably means the staff was guessing at the weight and not actually weighing them. If the charts indicate an erratic change in eating habits, it probably means that the employee is guessing at their intake or has not been properly trained to identify the quantity of intake. When a person dies or has complications due to malnutrition, this is an important aspect of the records.

In the course of the investigation, the police department records should be reviewed as well. Each jurisdiction has different restrictions on their records and their accessibility as well as the ways in which they can access the records. Where possible, ask them to check the home by address for a period of at least one-year prior to the time the subject was in the facility through at least six months afterwards. Request that they search the records by pulling every police call made regarding the facility's physical address. Once you receive the list back, you will be able to check for those calls regarding abuse, disturbances, thefts and similar circumstances. These may further document that the home has a problem with abuse as well as identifying potential witnesses.

Besides pulling the police records by address, I would suggest that you check by the facility's name and the corporation name that owns the home and/or the family members that own the home. You may find out some information on the owners of the home regarding violations of moral turpitude, violations of laws or similar questionable records.

Another place to check is the county civil and criminal records as well as the assumed names. The county clerk's office typically handles the assumed name records and a check of these should tell you who actually owns the nursing home. The District Court Clerk should be contacted and a review of their civil records made. These records will reflect any lawsuits filed against the nursing home facility or the owners of the home. If any are found, the actual file should be reviewed to better determine the facts and parties involved. The records may also list employee's names and other witnesses who may be helpful to your case.

Once the civil records are checked, the District Court Clerk's criminal records should be reviewed to determine any criminal violations against the home or the owners. In addition to these, another good place to look is the deed/judgment records found in the County Clerk's office. On-line databases are also making much of this available. These records will reflect any judgments filed against the home from within the county or outside of the county. Just because the home is located in a particular county doesn't mean that the same county will be used to file the lawsuit. If another county is known to be more liberal, attorneys will also change the venue of the case. Once a judgment is awarded against the facility, the record is filed in the county deed/judgment records to insure that the judgment is honored.

A check of the State's Secretary of State's records and the State's Comptroller's office should also be researched. The Secretary of State will have records reflecting the corporation that owns the nursing home, the officers, addresses, date it was filed, charter number and whether or not they are currently in good standing with the State. The State Comptroller's records will have some of this information, but if they are not a corporation by some chance, the home will still have to have filed with the comptroller's office to obtain a state taxpayer I.D. number. They will also tell you whether or not the company is up to date and in good standing with their office. Again, much of this is available on-line. A good investigator will remember however, that anything obtained from the internet my need to be re-verified.

The hospital records should be obtained and reviewed to determine the course and reasons for treatment. These should be checked and corresponded with the facility and doctor's records. If the person died in the hospital, it should reflect the actual cause. The records should be reviewed for any information concerning abuse such as broken bones, bruises, lacerations and similar identifiers.

The medical examiner's office records should be obtained and reviewed as well if an autopsy was conducted. The reports need to be crosschecked to determine the medications found in the person's bodies (or lack of medicine), the bruises, broken bones or similar signs of abuse. The ultimate reason for death will also be noted and should be double-checked against the facility's and your client's reasons.

Another interesting note is the use of social security numbers to track down possible witnesses who have moved. In addition, if the administrator or an employee has a social security number that originated in another state, it would be wise to check with the licensing board of that state to see if they had to move due to disciplinary problems with the board. The social security prefixes are as follows:

Social Security Numbers & State Origin

001-003 NH	400-407 KY	530	NV
004-007 ME	408-415 TN	531-539	WA
008-009 VT	416-424 AL	540-544	OR
010-034 MA	425-428 MS	545-573	CA
035-039 RI	429-432 AR	574	AK
040-049 CT	433-439 LA	575-576	HI
050-134 NY	440-448 OK	577-579	DC
135-158 NJ	449-467 TX	580	Virgin Islands
159-211 PA	468-477 MN	581-584	Puerto Rico
212-220 MD	478-485 IA	585	NM
221-222 DE	486-500 MO	586	PI Pacific Islands*
223-231 VA	501-502 ND	587-588	MS
232-236 WV	503-504 SD	589-595	FL
237-246 NC	505-508 NE	596-599	Puerto Rico
247-251 SC	509-515 KS	600-601	AZ

252-260 GA	516-517 MT	602-626 CA
261-267 FL	518-519 ID	627-645 TX
268-302 OH	520 WY	646-647 UT
303-317 IN	521-524 CO	648-649 NM
318-361 IL	525 NM	
362-386 MI	526-527 AZ	
387-399 WI	528-529 UT	

*Guam, American Samoa, Philippine Islands, Northern Mariana Islands

650-699 unassigned, for future use
700-728 Railroad workers through 1963, then discontinued
729-799 unassigned, for future use
800-999 not valid SSNs.

Some sources have claimed that numbers above 900 were used when some state programs were converted to federal control, but current SSA documents claim no numbers above 799 have ever been used.

Social Security Numbers*

A Social Security Number (SSN) consists of nine digits, commonly written as three fields separated by hyphens: AAA-GG-SSSS. The first three-digit field is called the "area number". The central, two-digit field is called the "group number". The final, four-digit field is called the "serial number".

The process of assigning numbers has been changed at least twice. Until 1965, only half the group numbers were used. Before 1972, field offices assigned numbers; since 1972, the central office has assigned them all. The order in which numbers were assigned was changed in the 1972 transition. There may have been other changes, but it's difficult to get information on how things used to be done. In approximately 2012, this changed and the prefix no longer dictates where the number originated.

Area Numbers

The area numbers are assigned to geographical locations. They were originally assigned the same way that zip codes were later assigned (in particular, area numbers increase from east to west across the continental US as do the ZIP codes). Most area numbers were assigned according to state (or territorial) boundaries, although the series 700-729 was assigned to railroad workers regardless of location (this series of area numbers was discontinued in 1964 and is no longer used for new SSNs). Area numbers assigned prior to 1972 are an indication of the SSA office that originally issued the SSN. Since 1972 the area number in SSNs corresponds to the residence address given by the applicant on the application for the SSN.

In many regions the original range of area number assignments was eventually exhausted as population grew. The original area number assignments have been augmented as required. All of the original assignments were less than 585 (except for the 700-729 railroad worker series mentioned above). Area numbers of "000" have never been issued.

Group Numbers

The group number is not related to geography but rather to the order in which SSNs are issued for a particular area. Before 1965, only half the group numbers were used: odd numbers were used below 10 and even numbers were used above 9. In 1965 the system was changed so assignments continued with the low even numbers and the high odd numbers. So, group numbers for each area number are assigned in the following order:

1. Odd numbers, 01 to 09
2. Even numbers, 10 to 98
3. Even numbers, 02 to 08
4. Odd numbers, 11 to 99

Group codes of "00" aren't assigned

In each region, all possible area numbers are assigned with each group number before using the next group number. This means the group numbers can be used to find a chronological ordering of SSNs within a region. When new group numbers are assigned to a state, the old numbers are usually used up first.

SSA publishes a list every month of the highest group assigned for each SSN Area. For example, if the highest group assigned for area 999 is 72, then we know that the number 999-04-1234 is an invalid number because even Groups under 9 have not yet been assigned.

Serial Numbers

Serial numbers are assigned in chronological order within each area and group number as the applications are processed. Serial number "0000" is never used. Before 1965, when number assignment was transferred from field offices to the central office, serial numbers may have been assigned in a strange order. (Some sources claim that 2000 and 7000 series numbers were assigned out of order. That no longer seems to be the case.) Currently, the serial numbers are assigned in strictly increasing order with each area and group combination.

Invalid SSNs

Any SSN conforming to one of the following criteria is an invalid number:

1. Any field all zeroes (no field of zeroes is ever assigned).
2. First three digits above 740

A pamphlet entitled "The Social Security Number" (Pub. No. 05-10633) provides an explanation of the SSN's structure and the method of assigning and validating Social Security numbers.

This description of the structure of the Social Security Number is based on messages written by Jerry Crow and Barbara Bennett. The information has been verified by its correspondence to the SSA's Program Operations Manual System (POMS) Part 01, Chapter 001, subchapter 01, which can be found at Federal Depository Libraries. (SSA Pub. No. 68-0100201.)

The Investigation in Theory

As in any investigation, the investigator should develop the fundamental who, what, when, where and why. Regarding the facility in question, the investigator should set out to obtain:

1) A copy of the facility's initial investigation, activities and findings. Remember that this a permanent and official record of the facility's actions, observations, and discoveries

2) The response of the facility once the investigation was completed

3) Written policies, procedures and manuals

4) The method they used to communicate the elements of the case, findings and responses

This information can be evaluated and analyzed to detect and identify patterns of conduct of the administration and facility. Sometimes the investigator can get too wrapped up in the case and the elements of the incident may not be properly spelled out and documented. The areas of the incident that should be specifically outlined include:

1) What exactly is the allegation? Write it down. This is the basis of your investigation and should be the guiding line that all information should be measured. Refer to it often. The investigator should compare the allegation to the definitions of caregiver misconduct and spell out where the violations line-up.

2) Make sure the information you are gathering is related to the incident and addresses the elements of the offense. It is easy to get off on rabbit trails that ultimately have nothing to do with the violations.

3) Document who was present at the time of the incident? (Victim, perpetrator, witness?)

4) Document who else might have information about the incident? (Other caregivers on duty, supervisors, visitors, maintenance or kitchen staff, social workers?)

5) Make sure to determine and list all persons who are connected in any way with the incident under investigation.

6) Specifically list where the incident took place (building number, hall number, room number, etc.).

7) Pin down the actual time (in addition to the date) that the incident happened as well as any special events taking place during that timeframe (birthday party, medical emergency, etc.).

8) Reconstruct the actual alleged incident and determine if this is logical and possible. Measure this against the written reports, witnesses or other sources.

9) Determine if there is any evidence, where it is located and how it is being preserved. Depending on when you become involved, you may have the opportunity to document the actual injuries, condition of the victim's clothing, furniture, etc.

10) Document the effect of the incident on the victim. It is important to photograph physical injuries but it is also important to document psychosocial effects such as fear, withdrawal, depression, etc. Make sure to document the victim's diagnosis and any physical limitations (dementia, physical or cognitive disabilities, etc.). In the event of neglect without injuries, document details that demonstrate the potential for harm.

11) Because the mindset of the caregiver and their "intent" are elements of criminal prosecution, attempt to document if the caregiver knew or should have known that their actions could have resulted in harm to the victim. Part of this can also be through reviewing the facilities policies and handouts.

  a) Did the facility's orientation materials or work rules state the definitions of misconduct?

  b) Does the facility have a written policy that spells out and prohibits caregiver misconduct?
  c) Is there any documentation the caregiver signed or other documents to prove the caregiver was aware of these definitions and rules?

  d) If neglect is the issue, how can you document that the caregiver's actions were negligent?

Develop the Scene:

If possible, draw a diagram and/or photograph the scene of the incident (e.g. the resident's room) and the location's relationship to the rest of the facility if you have access to the area. If not you will need to develop a diagram as conduct your investigation. You should include dimensions of the area and/or distances to other locations. This will help determine whether witnesses could actually see the incident from their vantage point. It will also help you visualize a witness's version of the incident. You may be able to go on the internet and search the appraisal district's records for the particular county in question. Often they provide a diagram of the buildings and will give an outline that can be a general starting point for the diagrams.

Develop a List of Persons to Interview

When reviewing documents, police reports, charts and other medical records, start making a list of potential interviewees. You may eliminate some of these as the investigation progresses but it will save you time later and help you to not overlook a witness. Some of the potential witnesses include:

1) Interview the reporter of the incident

2) Interview the victim if appropriate

3) Interview the accused *last* if the accused can be interviewed (not represented by an attorney, etc.).

4) Interview family members of other patients

5) Interview former employees of the facility as many times they may still have friends or relatives working at the facility in question.

6) Obtain written or recorded statements from witnesses

The setting of an interview can have a direct correlation to the success of the interview. Unfortunately the investigator will not always have control over this. Interviewing an employee away from the facility is imperative as they will not feel comfortable discussing the situation where the incident happened or where the management is located. Usually it is best to cold-call the person at their residence by not setting a pre-scheduled appointment. In setting an appointment, the person has time to cancel, think about the way they want to respond and to put up barriers. By catching them off-guard you will have a better and more truthful interview. It is important to have a photograph of the victim to show the interviewee to insure the discussion involves the correct patient.

Once you have conducted these preliminary fundamental investigative techniques, you can then turn your attentions to locating and interviewing possible witnesses.

CONDUCTING THE INTERVIEWS
Chapter Ten

The one trait that really sets this type of investigation apart from others is the investigator's personality and demeanor. For the most part, the investigator will be approaching people of minimum wages who often live in some of the more socio-economically depressed areas of the city. The success of the interview is many times determined by the manner in which the person is approached and the way that the investigator speaks to the subject.

As an example of this, I followed behind an investigator who had tried to interview almost twenty people who used to work at a nursing home. The investigator's report indicated that none of the subjects had anything remarkable to say, and in fact, he was only able to interview three or four of these people. My client, being dissatisfied with the results, asked me to handle this personally. I approached many of these subjects in a different manner and ended up getting some very useful statements that helped build the abuse case for the client.

The investigator has to remember that people are people, and as such, they do not want to be talked down to in a demeaning method. Many of the nursing home employees will tell you that they didn't like the administrators of the facility because they always talked down to them and made them feel subordinate to them. Position wise, they were subordinates, but as a person they were not. This is the same type of response you will get if you try to patronize the subject. These people are not ignorant, and they will recognize any insincerity for what it is. For the most part, you have just a few sentences in which to grab the person's attention. In those few sentences, you have to tell the subject what it is you are doing, what you want of them and convince them that you do not pose a threat to them. It is always good to smile while doing this as it helps put the person at ease with you.

I usually start out by stating that "I am working for "Jane Doe's" family who believes that she was neglected and abused while at ABC Nursing Home. I understand that you used to work there and I would like your help in determining if what we have heard is correct. If possible, I would like to take a few minutes of your time and ask you some simple questions." I then tell them that we have already talked to other people that have told us some of the things that occurred at the facility and we simply need to confirm that these things actually did or didn't happen. It is important that you downplay their involvement in any future court proceedings as most people will not want to get involved. If they ask about this, you may tell them that these things usually settle out of court, but all employees who worked there during that time could possibly be witnesses.

Once you get the person to agree to talk to you, ask them if you can record the conversation so that taking notes does not distract you. Most will not have any objection, and if they do, remind them that if they are one of the "luck" ones that gets called to court, they will probably have to give a deposition anyway. I usually explain that this is a way for the attorneys to find out what they know before they actually have to be called into court. I suggest that you take a little time and chit-chat with them a little so they will not be so defensive and will be more willing to open up to you. Once you are ready to get into the questions, the following are just some that should be asked:

1) Please state your correct name, home address and date of birth.

2) Mr./Mrs. (name), you don't understand that I am recording this conversation, correct?

3) Mr./Mrs. (name), I do have your permission to record this conversation, correct?

4) OK, thank you. Today's date is _____ and this conversation concerns (client/patient's name).

5) I know that you worked at the nursing home, but I am unsure of the actual dates, can you remember when you worked there?

6) What was your job description?

7) What shift did you work?

8) Did you work a particular hall or wing at the nursing home?

9) On the hall/wing that you worked on, was there a specific type of patient on this hall (medical)?

10) On a typical shift, how many aides usually worked?

11) In your opinion, was this enough (aides) to get the job done correctly?

12) Was calling in sick or employees just not showing up for work a problem?

13) On a typical shift, how many license vocational nurses (LVN's) were there on duty?

14) How many registered nurses (RN's) worked a typical shift?

15) Do you remember the name of the Director of Nurses (DON)?

16) Was there an Assistant Director of Nurses (ADON)?

17) What was the ADON's name?

18) Do you recall the administrator's name?

19) Did you see any of the administrators in the halls very much, or did they staff in their offices most of the time (mainly applies to day shift)?

20) Do you remember (name of client/patient)?

21) Was (name of patient) what you would consider a problem patient?

22) Did (name of patient) eat regularly?

23) Did you have to hand-feed (name of patient)?

24) Do you remember if the patient normally ate all of their meal or just a portion?

25) For the patients in general, was there a supplemental meal offered or available if they didn't eat what they were given?

26) In your opinion, did they offer enough food to the patients?

27) In your opinion, was the food eatable, in essence, would you eat it?

28) Did you ever see anyone take food away from a patient as a source of punishment?

29) Did you ever see or hear any employee threaten to shove the food down a patient's throat if they didn't eat?

30) When the food was served, was it served hot or cold?

31) Were bedsores a problem in your opinion?

32) Did you find many patients who were wet and laying in their own urine?

33) Did the nursing home have an odor of urine?

34) Do you recall finding many dried rings on the sheets where the person had obviously laid in their own urine until it had dried?

35) Did the facility use adult diapers?

36) Do you feel that the patients were checked less when they were in an adult diaper?

37) Did the nursing home have a policy regarding how often the patients were supposed to be checked and turned (usually every 2 hours)?

38) Did the employees stick to this or did they get busy doing other things?

39) When the employees turned and handled the patients, did they usually do it by themselves or did they have help?

40) Was help available if you needed it when turning a patient?

41) Did you ever see patients get handled roughly?

42) Did you ever see what has been referred to as "slam dunking" a patient when someone took the patient out of a wheel chair and tossed them into bed?

43) Do you remember any patient complaining about being handled roughly?

44) Are you aware of any situations of physical abuse?

45) Did you ever know of an employee who was disciplined or terminated because of the way they handled a patient?

46) When an employee was terminated, did you ever know of them to get re-hired by the facility later?

47) When you saw something that you knew was wrong, did you report it to the charge nurse or administrators?

48) Did the supervisors take the report seriously and was any action taken?

49) If they failed to act on your information, did you and the other employees stop telling them since you knew it would not be taken care of?

50) How many showers and/or baths did the facility have?

51) Do you think that there was enough to give every patient a bath?

52) Did you ever know of an employee to turn on the shower and act like they were giving the person a bath without actually putting them in it?

53) Were there enough towels and wash-clothes?

54) Did the employees usually wash their hands after dealing with each patient?

55) Were gloves worn by employees on a regular basis?

56) Were gloves supplied so that they could be worn?

57) Did you ever come in and find the call light buttons moved away from the patient?

58) Was it a regular occurrence for the call lights to be moved?

59) Did the employees respond to the call lights in a timely manner?

60) Were you ever aware of a patient being placed into a physical restraint without a doctor's order?

61) Were the restraints loosened and checked every two hours?

62) Did you ever know of a chemical restraint to be given to a patient to quiet them down without a doctor's order?

63) Did you ever know of an employee to give other employees medicine?

64) Did you ever see someone dispensing medication that was not licensed to do so?

65) Were you aware of any employees who were not to drink alcohol on the job or come to work intoxicated?

66) Were you aware of any employees who used drugs on the job or who came to work on drugs?

67) Was theft a problem in the facility (thefts from patients)?

68) Were the doors locked after normal working hours on a regular basis?

69) Did you ever know of any patient who wondered off from the home?

70) Were there any situations where someone off the street entered the home and caused trouble?

71) Did you ever see any of the employees sleeping on the job?

72) Did you ever see any of the employees watching TV on the job?

73) Were patients left in wheelchairs for long periods of time?

74) Were patients in wheelchairs checked on a regular basis?

75) Were you ever told or aware of anyone else ever being told to not report abuse?

76) Did you ever see someone intentionally failing to complete the charts or intentional miss-document information?

77) Did you ever see charts that were not completely filled out?

78) Have you ever been told to fill in charts even though you were not the person that gave the treatment?

79) Were you ever told to falsify the charts or other documents?

80) Were you ever present when the State came in for an inspection?

81) Did it appear that the nursing home knew in advance that the inspection was coming?

82) Did you see additional employees working during the inspection that were not usually working?

83) Were there any additional time cards put out with people's names on them who didn't even work there to make it look like they had more employees working?

84) Were there new supplies put out during the State's visit that were not usually there?

85) Do you know what the results of the inspections were?

86) Do you know if the State ever conducted an inspection based on a specific complaint?

87) Do you know of any families that have gotten irritated at the nursing home?

88) Do you know of anyone else that we should talk to?

89) When you changed a patient's dressings, did you initial the tape or dressing?

90) Were you ever aware of times when you came in and the dressing on the patient was the same as the day before?

91) When you first were hired, did anyone "train" you or walk around with you to give you an orientation?

92) Were you aware of any employees that were notified certified or licensed?

93) Were there any problems with the facility itself such as a roof that leaked when it rained?

94) Did the facility have the needed equipment necessary to properly treat the patients?

95) Did the administration of the facility get upset when you called the doctor or hospital?

96) When a person died, did the doctor come to the facility in a timely manner?

97) Did you ever see the dietician at the facility?

98) Did you keep a notepad in your pocket while working to jot down notes on before you could get back to the charts?

99) If so, do you still have them?

100) Was the laundry done on a regular basis?

101) Did you ever know of any animals that were allowed to live at the facility?

102) Do you know of any employees that had criminal histories or questionable backgrounds?

103) Do you know if the facility checked with any of your references before you were hired?

104) In your opinion, on a scale of 1-10 (10 being the highest), what is your opinion of the facility?

105) Why?

106) Is there anything particular about the nursing home or any of the employees that really stands out in your mind?

107) Is there anything else that we haven't asked that you think we should know?

108) Just to reiterate, your do understand that this conversation was recorded and I did have your permission?

Through the questions and answers, you will discover additional questions that should be asked or certain areas that need to be more closely concentrated on. By covering these broad ranges, you should determine the character of the witness and others that you may need to interview.

If you have a questionable witness or even one that you consider a "star" witness, it is a good idea to conduct a background check on the subject to make sure that their testimony will not get discredited in court. If a star witness has a questionable background, it doesn't necessarily mean that you will not be able to use them, it simply means that you will have to have additional witnesses who will support their testimony.

COMMON DENOMINATORS IN ABUSE
Chapter Eleven

In most abuse cases involving caregivers, there are certain things that seem to be common in most of these cases. These tend to be a starting place for your interviews and train of thought. As you begin to investigate and uncover other information, you will probably find variations and extreme cases. However, you can count on the following being present in almost all facilities:

- The facility is short of staff on a regular basis. The facility will try to say that they schedule enough employees and that they can't help it when people call in sick or are on vacation. The obvious response is that they need to start with a greater number of employees, if that is the case, to insure that you end of with the number you actually need.

- The staff is seldom able to stick to the policy of checking on and rotating a person in bed to prevent pressure sores.

- The patients are regularly left to lie in their own urine for extended periods of time.

- There are lazy employees and there are good employees. The lazy employees are the ones that add to the problems and they are the ones who everyone will turn on and tell on.

- Every employee has seen something or some way in which a person is handled which they did not agree with. This may be a theft, someone handling a patient too roughly or someone else they consider inappropriate.

- Almost all nursing homes do not have sufficient supplies (which includes linens, etc…).

- All nursing homes know ahead of time when a State Inspection is coming.

- All nursing homes have something that they don't want made public.

- All nursing homes have disgruntled employees who will probably make great witnesses.

The following indicators do not signify abuse or neglect *per se*. They can be clues however, and thus helpful in assessing the older person's situation[25]. The physical assessment of abuse should be done by a physician or trained health practitioner.

<u>Physical Indicators</u>

- Injury that has not been cared for properly.

- Any injury incompatible with person's explanation.

- Pain on touching.

- Cuts, lacerations, puncture wounds.

- Bruises, welt, discoloration:

    o On both upper arms.

    o Clustered on trunk, but may be found over any area of the body.

    o Injury looks like an object.

    o Presence of old and new bruises at the same time.

- Dehydration and/or malnourishment without illness-related cause; loss of weight.

- Pallor.

- Sunken eyes, cheeks.

- Evidence of inadequate care (i.e., gross decubitus without adequate medical care).

- Evidence of inadequate or inappropriate use of medication.

25

http://fcs.tamu.edu/families/aging/elder_care/indicators_of_elder_abuse_and_ne
glect.php

- Absence of hair and/or hemorrhaging below scalp.

- Soiled clothing or bed.

- Burns – may be caused by cigarettes, caustics, acids, friction from ropes or chains; from confinement.

- Signs of confinement (tied to furniture, bathroom fixtures, locked in a room).

- Lack of bandages on injuries or stitches when indicated, or evidence of unset bones.

Injuries are sometimes hidden under the breasts or on other areas of the body covered by clothing. Repeated skin or other bodily injuries should be noted and careful attention paid to their location and treatment. Frequent use of the emergency room and/or hospital or health care "shopping" may also indicate physical abuse. The lack of necessary aids such as walkers, canes, bedside commodes; lack of necessities such as heat, food, water, and unsafe conditions in the home (no railings on stairs, etc.) may indicate abuse or neglect.

Behavioral Indicators

These behaviors in themselves, of course, do not indicate abuse or neglect. However, they may be clues to ask more questions and look beyond the obvious.

- Fear

- Withdrawal

- Depression

- Helplessness

- Resignation

- Implausible stories

- Confusion or disorientation

- Ambivalence/contradictory statements not due to mental dysfunction

- Anger

- Denial

- Non responsiveness

- Agitation, anxiety

Indicators from the Family/Caregiver

- The older person may not be given the opportunity to speak for him or herself or to see others without the presence of the caregiver (suspected abuser).

- Obvious absence of assistance attitudes of indifference or anger toward the dependent person.

- Family member or caregiver "blames" the older person (i.e., accusation that incontinence is a deliberate act).

- Aggressive behavior (threats, insults, harassment).

- Previous history of abuse to others.

- Problems with alcohol or drugs.

- Flirtations, coyness, etc. as indicators of possible inappropriate sexual relationship.

- Social isolation of family or isolation or restriction of activity of the older adult within the family unit.

- Conflicting accounts of incidents by the family, supporters, and victim.

- Unwillingness or reluctance to comply with service providers in planning for care and implementation.

- Withholding of security and affection.

Most nursing homes have families that may be willing to come forward and testify to the poor treatment a family member has received. Like in many cases, opportunity is an element of any crime. If a caregiver is accused of stealing from a patient, the opportunity would have to present itself. For someone to physically abuse a patient, the opportunity had to have been present. Identify if the accuser had the opportunity to have been alone with the patient and in a position to have abused the patient. On the midnight shift, the halls are more quiet, nurses try to catch up on paperwork and caregivers do a lot of monitoring of patients. On the dayshift, patients are given showers, clothes and bedding is changed and there is more activity in general. A caregiver walking by a room is less likely to pay attention to things in other rooms. The noise level is higher, family and friends are present and keeping up with specific activities of caregivers is harder. This increase in activity is a good cover for thefts, abuse or neglect.

Remembering these factors and directing your investigation towards these from the very beginning will lead to specific situations and witnesses that will help prove neglect and abuse.

Individuals who are faced with giving up their ability to take care of themselves often have to battle depression. While this is common, long periods of depression can be a sign of something more traumatic. Understanding common signs will help assess the situation more accurately:

Depression: Signs and Causes[26]

In the midst of losses, such as physical changes, death of friends or loved ones and reduction of income, older people may begin showing signs of depression. Some things to look for are:

a) inability to concentrate or make decisions,

---

[26] http://www.longtermcarelink.net/eldercare/the_caregivers_handbook.htm

b) lack of feelings of enjoyment, or enthusiasm even for doing those things that were favorites,

c) little interest in eating (causing weight loss) or changes in eating habits (overeating causing weight gain),

d) lack of interest in being with other people,

e) feeling unwanted and worthless, sometimes leading to the thought that life is not worth living,

f) sadness or crying spells for no apparent reason,

g) problems with sleeping (sleeplessness during the night or excessive sleep during most of the day),

h) feeling tired most of the time, regardless of adequate rest.

If older people brood about their unhappiness, much of their energy is focused on worry. Part of that worry may relate to the fear that they will become forgetful and unable to manage their affairs. This worry can lead down the path to more depression, which may cause physical problems. In exploring the cause of depression, the following questions should be asked:

Is there a physical or medical problem causing the depression?

a) Have there been changes in hearing, seeing, moving, or other body functions?

b) What social contact does the care-receiver have?

c) What are the opportunities for usefulness?

d) Is the older person getting proper nutrition?

e) What kind of mental stimulation is the person getting?

f) Is the focus entirely on the past or is there some enthusiasm about coming events?

g) Is there a possibility of reaction to medications?

h) Is there a dependency on alcohol or drugs?

Once these questions have been answered, steps can be taken to relieve the depression. It will take some work from both the caregiver and the care-receiver to change habits and routines. Prolonged depression causes biochemical changes in the brain, usually requiring treatment with medication. The doctor is a good person the contact to find help for treatment of depression. Other resources are County Mental Health Centers, psychologists, counselors or clergy.

Suicide Prevention:

Suicide among the elderly is a significant and ever increasing problem. Statistics show that:

- 27 percent of all suicides in San Diego county (1985-87) were committed by people 60 years of age and older.

- Nationally, elderly (65+ years) made up 12.3 percent of 1987 population and committed 21.0 percent of suicides.

- Elderly complete one suicide every 1 hour and 21 minutes, or each day 17.7 seniors committed suicide.

Unlike other segments of the population, the elderly do not often make threats or mention suicidal thoughts to others. Therefore, it is important that caregivers also know other warning signs:

a) Depression - feelings of sadness, hopelessness, a sense of loss and statements as "Life isn't worth living" are common before a suicide.

b) Chronic or terminal illness.

c) Withdrawal and isolation - suicidal people may pull away from family, friends and others close to them.

d) Behavior changes - sudden changes such as irritability, aggressiveness or changes in eating and sleeping habits can signal problems.

e) Making final arrangements - a suicidal person may give away valued possessions, making out a will, make a plan for suicide, or write a suicidal note in preparation.

f)   They may purchase weapons or stockpile medications.

Suicide can be prevented. If the person you care for shows any of the warning signs, you can:

1) Ask - don't be afraid to ask directly if the person is thinking about suicide. It is not a taboo subject. You will not be putting ideas into the person's head. It can be a relief to the suicidal person to talk openly about their feelings.

2) Listen - let the person express his/her feelings and concerns. Don't worry about saying the right things - just listen.

3) Show you care - tell the person you care and want to help. Take active steps to make sure the person is safe; remove weapons, pills, etc., and stay with him/her.

4) Get help - make sure the suicidal person gets in contact with a professional counselor or other helpful person who will know what to do. Have the suicidal person call (suicide prevention/crisis intervention Hotline in your community. Telephone numbers for such local resources should be at the front of your telephone

5) directory.) A crisis counselor can help figure out the best way to handle the situation and give referrals to other resources.

Death and Dying Interventions Elderly terminally ill encounter anxiety and fear regarding death:

a)   fear of the process of dying; will there be pain?

b)   fear of losing control; will I be at another's mercy?

c)   fear of letting go; I cannot leave family and friends to an uncertain future.

d)   fear of seeing how others will avoid me.

e)   fear of losing my caregiver; will he/she be turned off emotionally to me?

f)   fear of the unknown after death.

g) fear that my "life's script" has been meaningless, unfulfilled, a waste.

You may wish to ease these fears through an open discussion of these fears and by intervening. Regarding the death process, a "faith system" may be of great help. If you can get the person involved in their religious faith, the subject of death is well covered.

Regarding their fear of letting go and isolation, assist the person in getting their "house in order." This entails a will, funeral arrangements, burial plot, etc. Also attempt to have the person and family involved discuss the situation.

Regarding meaninglessness of one's life, have the person do a "Life Script," whereby they writes all the good things done for others, all accomplishments, etc. Then discuss with the person that and enforce the fact that they had a full life that positively impacted others.

JOB DESCRIPTIONS
Chapter Twelve

One of the basic criteria for working caregiver abuse cases I having an understanding of what jobs there are in a facility and what tasks these positions normally perform. Some of these positions may have duties that cross-over into the job descriptions of another position; however, the following is designed for an over-view of jobs:

> Director of Nurses: Commonly called the "DON", this job is normally held by a Registered Nurse. The Director of Nurses is just that, they direct other nurses. This position requires the DON to over-see the daily operation of the facility, to make sure that the paperwork is done and that the facility is ran with the least amount of problems as possible. Because this is a position of management, many of the employees will often vent their frustrations and anger towards the DON. It is common for witnesses to "slam" the DON when talking about the nursing home. For this reason, the investigator has to weed through the statements to determine if there is simply a personality conflict or if there is something deeper and more significant. In addition, the DON is often caught in the middle. Whenever the administrators have a problem, they blame it on the DON. Likewise, the employees blame the DON for their troubles.

For the most part, interviewing the DON will not provide you with any major revelations. The DON is a professional manager and knows that any information they provide is sure to discredit their management. In addition, many of the things that go on at a facility walk a thin line of criminal activity and the DON knows that they could be held legally responsible for anything done under their direction. At the very least, many of these things breach the ethical standards of the profession and they may be aware that their testimony may jeopardize their license.

Interviewing the DON requires a great deal of patience and careful consideration. The questions must be phrased in a manner that does not appear to be an accusation of the DON. When talking to a person in this position, it is often a good idea to talk about their credentials and former job experience to enable them to "justify" their position of authority to the investigator. The DON then feels a little more secure because they think the investigator will not point the finger at them since they have so much education and experience. The DON has to be pampered a little more than most. If you have been told some good things about the facility or the DON themselves, it is a good idea to indicate that you have been told that they were fair with their employees, they never yelled at their subordinates or something similar. In this way, you do the old "brown nose" trick, which is effective because it once again helps to settle the nerves of the subject.

It is important when interviewing the DON (or any other witness for that matter) that you remain as unbiased as possible in your comments, especially when recording the conversation. It is OK to agree with a statement, but you definitely do not want to come off as being shown to be pro-facility when you are trying to find facts against the facility.

In their job as a DON, they probably do the least amount of actual nursing. Sometimes they have some staff that call in sick and are left short-handed, and when this happens, they are forced into filling in. During questioning, you should ask them how often this occurred. If it was on a regular basis, it further demonstrates under-staffing. In addition, if the DON is having to fill-in a lot, their jobs are not getting done like they should.

In the liberalist form, a DON may get involved in helping pass out medicine, start G-tubes, and rotate a patient or other functions commonly done by others. However, in the strictest form, the DON usually doesn't have time for most hands-on nursing activity. The questions directed towards the DON should therefore have this in mind. Many of the questions asked of the DON should deal with facility policies, procedures and paperwork. These are the things the DON will be the most up-to-date on and is the one responsible form man of these issues.

Although the DON is usually a registered nurse, sometimes you will find a LVN filling the position.

➢ Assistant Director of Nurses: Often referred to as the ADON, they are usually an R.N. or an L.V.N., depending on the size of the facility. This person fills in for the DON on their off days and usually works different shifts and schedules. This person is probably not going to tell you much because they are caught between the DON, the administration and the employees.

➢ Registered Nurse: Commonly referred to as an R.N. The Director of Nurses will most likely be an R.N. However, there is usually at least one R.N. on duty per shift at the facility above and beyond the DON. The R.N. directly involves herself with dispensing medicines, charting, contacting doctors, contacting families, reviewing patient's progress and determining courses of action for those patients who have difficulties.

Once again, the R.N. is one of the highest-ranking positions in the facility and they have the most to lose if they and the nursing home are found negligent. The R.N. will typically have a 4-year degree in nursing and should be treated with the respect deserved. Questions directed at the R.N. should involve issues of reporting such as what is their procedure when an employee notifies them of possible abuse or when someone is believed to be stealing from the patients. You should get more detailed with specific questions including such things as how often do you get these kinds of reports, how many employees have been investigated for suspicion of abuse, how many times were the police called, and were written reports made and similar questions.

The R.N. is also the person that you should direct questions dealing with issues surrounding adherence to turning patients, cleaning patients, feeding of patients and related questions. Always remember to be a little sympathetic towards the R.N. by acknowledging that they can't be everywhere and that you know they have a difficult job.

Unfortunately, the DON and the R.N.'s are probably going to provide some of the least useful information. Outside of policies and procedures, they are not going to incriminate themselves and since they are in management, you probably will not "break open the case" based on your conversations with them.

➢ The Licensed Vocational Nurse: Commonly referred to as an L.V.N. is typically a position that required an associate degree (2 years of college). This position is being phased out in many states. However, their original intention was to be kind of an assistant to the R.N., taking many of their responsibilities over to allow the R.N. to focus on the more critical areas of their nursing functions. The L.V.N.'s that you encounter will probably be more likely to open up to your questions that the R.N.'s. They are a semi-management position and therefore know enough about the goings-on at the facility to be of assistance to you in forming the adherence of the facility to common industry procedures. The L.V.N. is more closely related to the other employees and therefore usually knows more about the individual employees and their problems.

The L.V.N. has a more hands-on approach to daily care of the patients. They get more involved with each patient and assist the aides in many of their tasks. The investigator should therefore feel comfortable asking the L.V.N. more specific questions about the care given the patients. When approached right, they may be willing to tell you information on both the management and the employees that can be helpful.

➢ Certified Nurse's Aide: Commonly referred to as a C.N.A. or just simply as an aide. These are the people that do all the dirty work. They are responsible for washing and bathing the patients, feeding them, changing sheets, helping them in and out of bed and for the general needs of the person. They are the "front-line" workers who talk to their patients on a regular basis. These are also the same people who are most likely to abuse and neglect the patients.

Unfortunately, the aides get paid minimum wage, or just slightly higher. Their education is limited and they often have a struggling personal life. Having financial and personal problems at home, when coupled with the stress of a combative patient, may be more than they can deal with. I am not saying that it is right, but at least you see how the situation can escalate.

The aides are the ones who will be the most likely to talk to you and tell you the way it really is. They will tell you the names of others that they knew of who actually abused patients. The aides will also be very candid about the patients, the management and the families of the patients. If you want to know if the family ever visited their family member, they can tell you. If you want to know who the person most likely to abuse a patient was, they can tell you. These are the people who gossip among themselves and who see things they are not intended to see. The questions listed in Chapter 7 are the ones specifically designed for the aides.

Unfortunately, the aides that leave the facilities are also the ones that will be the hardest to find because of their lifestyles. Because they make very little money, they often move around a lot, which makes finding them in the first place somewhat difficult. As a footnote on this subject, it should be remembered that they often bounce around from one nursing home to another. You can probably call the nursing homes that are the closest to the one they worked at and find them working at one of these. For more information on locating people, you can read "Private Investigating Made Easy," also by Kelly Riddle.

A good line of questioning to get into with these subjects involves licensing. Some of the facilities will attempt to train and license their own aides but for one reason or another, never complete the training courses. Often, there will be aides working who are not certified or who are in training but are allowed to work by themselves without supervision.

➤ Medication Aide: Often referred to as the "med. aide," is a position which assists in dispensing medicine to the patients to help alleviate the work load of the L.V.N. or R.N. For the most part, this aide will typically have very little to say because they are going to tell you that they didn't spend much time with the patients and were just in and out of their rooms long enough to give them their medicine. Every once in a while though, you will find one that took time to talk to the patients and who took time to talk to other aides. These are the ones that will be most useful in an investigation. The aide is usually not going to confess that she gave medicine to another regular aide to give to a patient. They may tell you that they did this occasionally because they had a patient who would not take the medicine for them and they had to call the C.N.A. in to give the patient their medicine. The med. Aid is also not going to admit to giving a patient's medicine to another patient to knock the patient out.

The med. aide has to undergo specific training for the handling of drugs and their uses which allows them to be registered as a medication aide. A regular C.N.A. should not be dispensing narcotics unless they are a med. aide. The med. aide can tell you information about the general characteristics of the nursing home, the cleanliness of patients, bruises and marks on patients and things such as this.

Even though some of the employees such as R.N.'s and med. aides do not typically give you the best testimony, they should still be interviewed as they have good general knowledge of the facility and they may be the exception to the rule.

➤ Housekeeping: The housekeeping department is the one which "takes care of the house." They wash the sheets, towels, and washrags and perform cleaning functions throughout the facility. They can give you a good idea of how "soiled" the bed sheets are when they go to wash them and whether this is a problem in the facility. These people are in and out of the rooms and they see and hear a lot. You never know who will be the key witness and they should therefore also be interviewed. An interesting note is that often, these people will have relatives who work in the facility as aides or nurses.

➤ Maintenance: The maintenance department is responsible for fixing and keeping things running. Talking with some of these subjects can tell you whether or not the facility had insufficient equipment, enough bathroom facilities or other problems that directly affect the care of the patient. Like housekeeping, they are also in and out of patient's rooms and they have the potential to see and hear a lot as well.

➤ Administrators: The nursing home facility administrators may or may not be a licensed R.N. Sometimes, the person graduates out of nursing and into full-blown management. The administrators are responsible for the hiring and firing, paying taxes and payroll, ordering supplies, staying in compliance with health regulations and other managerial tasks. These are the people that you don't even want to talk to unless under a subpoena and deposition setting.

This is just a broad over-view of the positions commonly found in a nursing home facility. They may have additional, specific positions designed for their direct needs, but for the most part, these are the ones you will encounter.

COMMON MEDICAL TERMINOLOGY
Chapter Thirteen

When conducting caregiver abuse cases, it is helpful to understand some of the medical terms and how they come to bear in the investigation. For obvious reasons, the information will be discussed in lay-terms:

❏ Sepsis: This is a term that according to the Mayo Clinic Medical Reference guide is "an infection in the blood." The infection usually comes about due to a bed sore that has progressed into an infection. Bedsores, also known as pressure sores or decubitus ulcers, sometimes develop on weight-bearing parts of the body, especially where the bones are near the skin (in particular, the hips, shoulder blades, elbows, base of the spine, knees, ankles and heels). In some individuals, just a few hours of contact pressure can be enough to initiate a bedsore.

❏ Bedsore: Also known as a pressure sore comes about from having a person lay in one position too long and the body causing sores at points where the pressure is exerted against the bed. A bedsore begins as a reddened, sensitive patch of skin and progresses to a sore or ulcer. It may or may not be painful. Treatment of a bedsore requires the attention of a nurse or physician, and healing may take a long time. Prevention is therefore the best approach. Bedsores may be prevented by frequent re-positioning and by encouraging the bedridden person to move regularly to keep pressure from building on one spot. If the person cannot move alone, the aide or other person should assist them and a change of position should be conducted at least every 2 hours. The use of pillows or foam wedges to shift the load of a heavy or paralyzed individual is also recommended. Splints placed at pressure points are also helpful along with special anatomically shaped cushions, such as those in wheelchairs, can be placed in the bed to distribute weight more evenly. Other helpful devices are synthetic sheepskin bed pads, air mattresses and "egg-crate" pads. For more severe cases, a person should have a bed cradle that raises the weight of the covers off of the body and creates a tent-like structure.

Changes in bedding, drying thoroughly after baths, a balanced diet and exercise are important for avoiding bedsores. Even the bed-bound person can exercise using special techniques and movements of joints by others that will help prevent bedsores.

❑ Ulcer: a common term associated with bedsores. For more information, see the topic on bedsores or sepsis.

❑ Decubitus Ulcer: The term that designates a pressure sore that has progressed into an open wound. For more information, see the topic on bedsores or sepsis.

❑ Anemia: Occasionally, an anemia can develop as the result of a chronic disease. The important groups of chronic diseases most often associated with anemia include; chronic inflammation such as rheumatoid arthritis; uremia (as in kidney failure); acute chronic infections and decubitus ulcers. Anemia or chronic disease is curable only if the underlying disorder is cured or made less severe. Because the anemia causes a low platelet count, easy bruising and bleeding occur. This in turn, leaves that patient vulnerable to bacterial infection.

❑ Bleeding Disorders: Disruption of the body's elaborate process by which blood clots form are called bleeding disorders.

❑ Stasis Dermatitis: This is characterized by thickening and itching of the skin at the ankles. Varicose veins, and other chronic conditions in the legs involving vessels other than arteries, can lead to build-up of fluid (edema) in tissues beneath the skin. As a result, these areas are poorly nourished by blood and become fragile. Because ankles have less supportive tissues, they tend to be the most likely place for this to occur. The skin may become inflamed and open ulcers may develop which heal very slowly.

❑ Neurodermatitis: Often the condition, Lichen simplex chronicus is used interchangeably, they are not the same. These skin conditions consist of small flat growths of various sizes with definite margins that have become thickened and leather-like. Lichen simplex chronicus is usually the result of something (often a tight garment or sheet) that rubs or scratches an area of your skin. The leads to thickening of the skin, which in turn, produces itching and thus encourages more rubbing and scratching.

Although you may not need all of these, if you investigate nursing home cases, you will hear and read these and other terms. Understanding their meaning and application to your case will assist in a successful investigation. In addition, having a working knowledge of medical prefixes will aid in this as well. Enclosed are a list of common medical combining terms:

- Acr: pertaining to an extremity

- Bio: pertaining to life

- Cardi: pertaining to the heart

- Chole: pertaining to bile

- Derm: pertaining to the skin

- Enter: pertaining to intestines

- Hem: pertaining to the blood

- Kopr: pertaining to feces

- My: pertaining to muscles

- Myc: pertaining to fungi

- Oste: pertaining to bones

- Path: pertaining to disease

- Pneum: pertaining to the lung/air

- Pyel: pertaining to the pelvis

- Rach: pertaining to the spine

- Salping: pertaining to a tube

- Trache: pertaining to the trachea

Some of the common prefixes that are used include"

- Circum: around

- Contra: opposed

- Ecto: outside

- Epi: above or upon

- Hemi: half

- Hyper: above, excess of something

- Hypo: under, deficiency of something

- Infra: below

- Inter: between

- Intra: within

- Macro: large

- Micro: small

- Mycet: fungus

- Para: wrong, irregular, in the neighborhood of

- Poly: many

- Pseud: false

- Tachy: fast

It may be advantageous for the investigator to take some continuing education classes related to medicine. An investigator that has an EMT or related background this will provide a better opportunity to be an asset in these types of cases.

MEDICAL CHARTS
Chapter Fourteen

While conducting the investigation, you should have the opportunity to review the charts that pertained to your client while at the nursing home facility. First, you need to know what the charts are as well as why they are used. The normal charts that you may see are as follows:

✓ Intake Report: This is the document that the facility uses when a person is first admitted into their facility. It will have the patient's identifying information on it as well as certain indicators such as weight, blood-pressure, pulse, medical conditions, allergies, current medicines, doctor, emergency names and numbers and similar information. This document may be of importance as it will prove that they knew about a certain condition that they later deny. It may also show the condition of that patient at the time they entered the facility versus their last stages.

✓ Input-Output Chart: These charts are usually kept with the patient's charts at the nursing station. However, sometimes, the aides will tape a copy of this to the bathroom door to remind them to fill it out and to make sure that they do so. The chart is designed to keep a record of how much the person takes in during the day (such as juice, water, etc...). In addition, the staff is supposed to log the volume that the person outputs through using the bathroom. These charts are important as they will show a number of things such as (1) how often the person was checked (2) if the person had a normal input-output (3) if the person's input-output was characteristic of someone with their medical conditions (4) if the person was actually getting the medicine prescribed as these drugs often increase the fluids required and similar information of value.

✓ The Patient's Charts: These are supposed to be at the nurse's station at all times and regular notes should be a part of the file. As the staff checks on the patient, makes changes to their diet, discover bruises, observe changes in the patient's feces and find similar information involving the patient, they are supposed to be "charted" or logged in the chart. If the doctor was called and a change of orders was given, the change should be documented in the records. Unfortunately, this is one of the items that often gets over-looked because it takes time and effort to do. Often, the staff will put only the most significant information in the charts. Later, when an issue is made of the charts, they will suddenly remember and indicate that they just didn't have time to put it in the chart. The bottom line to this is, "if it ain't in the chart, it didn't happen."

✓ Medication Chart: This chart is designed to track the medication of the particular patient. The date, time, drug, dosage and similar information are supposed to be on the chart. A review of the records should be made to insure that (1) the medicine was being given, (2) that the right medicine was being given to the right person, (3) that the right dosage was being given, (4) that the medicine was being given at the required time, (5) that the person giving the medicine was licensed to do so and similar tactics.

✓ Daily Care Chart: These charts are designed to remind the staff of all the items of care that need to be given to the patient. This includes baths, skin care, grooming, exercise, and the patient's weight, feeding and additional personal care items. These charts are important because these are the ones that most often get over-looked. These charts are the ones that will show that the facility was caring for the person even after they were in the hospital or deceased. Very seldom do nursing homes actually weigh the patient on a daily basis. The staff will usually take the weight from the week before and just estimate the person's weight. The problem with this is that they take the weight from the week before, and the week before and the week before. It doesn't take long for a fluctuation in the person's weight to have occurred and should have sent up red flags if they had actually weighted the subject.

✓ Nurse's Notepads: The aides and nurses are taught to stick a small notepad in their pockets when they are at work. Many times, the employees will not have time to go back to the nurse's desk to write something in the chart and they write it in their personal notebook. Hopefully, the information will get transferred to the patient's chart at a later date. When interviewing former employees, ask if they kept their notepads. If they did, ask to make a copy of it so you can check their notes against the charts. I have come across nurses who have drawers full of notepads and just jarring their memory may be what is needed to open up the case.

These are the basic charts that you will find in a facility pertaining to the patient. Sometimes they will be called something a little different or there may be additional charts, but you need to understand these to complete a successful investigation.

AN OVERVIEW OF NURSING
Chapter Fifteen

Nursing, which is commonly known as the caring for of the sick, wounded or infirm, has a dramatic impact on the patient and their progress. Good nursing for someone sick can hasten recovery, prevent complications and maybe even save a life. Often, just keeping the patient as comfortable as possible and in good spirits is of great importance. A good nurse carefully observes the patient and accurately reports to their supervisor or doctor what they have noted.

The nurse should help prepare a room where the patient will be, making sure that it is clean and properly ventilated, with all harmful obstacles out of the way. "Nursing" in general, pertains to the aides, nurses, doctors, administrators, housekeeping and maintenance personnel all working together for the common good of the patient. This includes some of the following items:

- Beds: changing the bed each day (or more frequent when needed) and washing the patient daily. The bed should be out of any drafts from windows or air conditioning units. Rubber sheeting to protect the mattress and control fungus is important. Another common device is the "draw-sheet" which can be improvised by folding bed sheets of regular size to fit the middle of the bed. It extends to about the shoulders to the knees and is easily changed. Extra pillows are many uses in preventing pressure sores. Placing one rolled at the foot of the bed under the blanket eliminates pressure on the toes. Placing a pillow under the patient's knees also helps to take tension off of joints.

- Bathing Skills: Simple bathing of a person and brushing of their teeth generally aids in the recovery of the patient. An often-overlooked item is the method in which a patient is washed. If bedridden, washing and drying only one part of the body at a time, while leaving the rest of the body covered is important. This not only keeps their temperature constant, but maintains their dignity. Bathing not only makes the person feel better, but also helps the recovery by removing wastes thrown off by the skin.

- Room temperature: the temperature of the room is another often-overlooked item. The temperature should be kept constant and moderate and air should not blow directly on the patient.

- Assessments – this is an area where a good investigator can pick up where the nurses have failed. Part of their responsibilities includes checking the patient's vital signs, pupils, lungs, skin condition, weight and overall condition. Often the caregiver will simply looks to see what the shift before them entered on the charts and copy it. When this is done day after day, changes in the patient's condition is not noticed. As technology gets better so does assessments as much of this is done electronically. However, technology costs money and not all facilities have up-to-date or enough equipment.

- Medication Dispensing – insuring that patients get their medication and the *right* medication seems easy and logical. In many facilities there are Certified Nursing Assistants that are "medication aides." The R.N. is supposed to oversee the dispensing of the medication. Many times the medication aide will take the pills in a small paper cup and take into the patient's room. If the patient doesn't immediately take the medicine, the aide may get called out to help another aide or patient or get distracted. The patient may therefore not end up taking their medicine. There are also documented cases where the C.N.A. gave a patient's medicine to a different patient to "knock them out" as they are a patient requiring too much attention.

- Wound Care – in facilities with bed-ridden patients this is extremely important. If a patient lays in their own urine it starts to break down the skin condition. If a patient is not rotated every few hours they develop bedsores. Often caregivers get busy and do not attend to the wounds and leave it for the following shift. It doesn't take long for the wounds to turn into a major health issue.

- Notifications – part of the job of caregivers is to notify their supervisor, doctor or family members of concerns. It is especially important for doctors to receive timely information to prevent the condition turning into a life threatening issue.

- Education – patients and family members often do not have any idea about what to expect, how they can help or what they should and should not do. Caregivers are in a unique position to help the patient and family members by answering questions and giving them needed information.

These are just a few of the most commonly over-looked items that need to be considered during the investigation. The P.I. should line-up information against these responsibilities and document variations from standards and procedures.

STATE AGENCIES
Chapter Sixteen

When conducting these types of investigations, you will certainly need to know the licensing requirements and how to obtain the records already discussed in the book. To start with, here is a list of state agencies:

MEDICAL BOARDS (MED*)

Alabama: Alabama Medical Board
P.O. Box 36101
Montgomery, Alabama 36101

Alaska: Alaska Medical Board
P.O. Box D
Juneau, Alaska 99811

Arizona: Arizona Medical Board
3601 West Camelback Road
Phoenix, Arizona 85015

Arkansas: Arkansas Medical Board
P.O. Box 102
Harrisburg, Arkansas 72432

California: California Medical Board
1426 Howe Avenue
Sacramento, California 95825

Colorado: Colorado Medical Board
1560 Broadway
Denver, Colorado 80202

Connecticut: Connecticut Medical Board
150 Washington Street
Hartford, Connecticut 06106

Delaware: Delaware Medical Board
P.O. Box 1401
Dover, Delaware 19903

District of Columbia: D. C. Medical Board
605 G. Street, NW
Washington, D.C. 20001

Florida: Florida Medical Board
                    1940 North Monroe Street
                    Tallahassee, Florida 32399

Georgia: Georgia Medical Board
                    166 Pryor Street, Southwest
                    Atlanta, Georgia 30303

Hawaii: Hawaii Medical Board
                    P.O. Box 3469
                    Honolulu, Hawaii 96801

Idaho: Idaho Medical Board
                    280 North 8th Street
                    Boise, Idaho 83720

Illinois: Illinois Medical Board
                    320 West Washington
                    Springfield, Illinois 62786

Indiana: Indiana Medical Board
                    One American Square
                    Indianapolis, Indiana 46282

Iowa: Iowa Medical Board
                    1209 West Court Avenue
                    Des Moines, Iowa 50319

Kansas: Kansas Medical Board
                    235 Southwest Topeka Boulevard
                    Topeka, Kansas 66603

Kentucky: Kentucky Medical Board
                    400 Sherbon Lane
                    Louisville, Kentucky 40207

Louisiana: Louisiana Medical Board
                    830 Union Street
                    New Orleans, LA 70112

Maine: Maine Medical Board
                    State House, Room 137
                    Augusta, Maine 04333

Maryland: Maryland Medical Board
                    P.O. Box 2571
                    Baltimore, Maryland 21215

Massachusetts: Massachusetts Medical Board
                    10 West Street

Boston, Massachusetts 02111

Michigan: Michigan Medical Board
                  P.O. Box 30018
                  Lansing, Michigan 48909

Minnesota: Minnesota Medical Board
                  2700 University Avenue, West
                  Saint Paul, Minnesota 55114

Mississippi: Mississippi Medical Board
                  2688 Insurance Center Drive
                  Jackson, Mississippi 39216

Missouri: Missouri Medical Board
                  P.O. Box 4
                  Jefferson City, Missouri 65102

Montana: Montana Medical Board
                  1424 9th Avenue
                  Helena, Montana 59620

Nebraska: Nebraska Medical Board
                  P.O. Box 95007
                  Lincoln, Nebraska 68509

Nevada: Nevada Medical Board
                  P.O. Box 7238
                  Reno, Nevada 89510

New Hampshire: New Hampshire Medical Board
                  6 Hazen Drive
                  Concord, New Hampshire 03301

New Jersey: New Jersey Medical Board
                  28 West State Street
                  Trenton, New Jersey 08608

New Mexico: New Mexico Medical Board
                  P.O. Box 20001
                  Santa Fe, New Mexico 87504

New York: New York Medical Board
                  Empire State Plaza, Room 3023
                  Albany, New York 12230

North Carolina: North Carolina Medical Board
                  1313 Navaho Drive
                  Raleigh, North Carolina 27609

North Dakota: North Dakota Medical Board
                418 East Broadway
                Bismarck, North Dakota 58501

Ohio: Ohio Medical Board
                77 South High Street
                Columbus, Ohio 43266

Oklahoma: Oklahoma Medical Board
                P.O. Box 18256
                Oklahoma City, Oklahoma 73154

Oregon: Oregon Medical Board
                620 Crown Avenue
                Portland, Oregon 97201

Pennsylvania: Pennsylvania Medical Board
                P.O. Box 2649
                Harrisburg, Pennsylvania 17105

Puerto Rico: Puerto Rico Medical Board
                P.O. Box 13969
                Santurce, Puerto Rico 00908

Rhode Island: Rhode Island Medical Board
                3 Capital Hill Road
                Providence, Rhode Island 02908

South Carolina: South Carolina Medical Board
                 Post Office Box 12245
                 Columbia, South Carolina 29211

South Dakota: South Dakota Medical Board
                1323 South Minnesota Ave.
                Sioux Falls, S.D. 57105

Tennessee: Tennessee Medical Board
                283 Plus Park Road
                Nashville, Tennessee 37247

Texas: Texas Medical Board
                P.O. Box 13562
                Austin, Texas 78711

Utah: Utah Medical Board
                P.O. Box 45802
                Salt Lake City, Utah 84145

Vermont: Vermont Medical Board

Pavillion Building, Room 100
Montpelier, Vermont 05609

Virginia: Virginia Medical Board
1601 Rolling Hills Drive
Richmond, Virginia 23229

Washington: Washington Medical Board
1300 Quince Street
Olympia, Washington 98504

West Virginia: West Virginia Medical Board
101 Dee Drive
Charleston, West Virginia 25311

Wisconsin: Wisconsin Medical Board
P.O. Box 8935
Madison, Wisconsin 53708

Wyoming: Wyoming Medical Board
2301 Central Avenue
Cheyenne, Wyoming 82002

Most state agencies are now on the internet and is a good source for verifying if the caregiver has a current license. You can also locate adverse ratings and reports on the facility in question.

INVESTIGATING ON BEHALF OF NURSING HOME FACILITIES
Chapter Seventeen

The medical community has not been receptive to self-policing and they are just now even beginning to acknowledge that it has a problem. Until they do, nothing serious will come of this issue, except large lawsuits. Like the half empty/half full scenario (one person says a glass is half full and the other says it is half-empty), there are two sides to every story. We all know that statistics can be presented in several different ways to sway the concept being presented. Although nursing home abuse is pretty cut and dry, anyone who has interviewed witnesses for very long can tell you that your approach and your questioning has a lot to do with the information obtained.

For instance, instead of telling the former nursing home employees that you already know a lot of the problems with the nursing home and you just want to see if they agree, there is a different approach if you are working for the "other side of the coin." In that situation, I would start off by telling the former employee that we understand that they were a good employee and that we know that they worked hard and tried to do the best they could while employed there. I would then tell them that a family is trying to "make a mountain out of a mole hill" and that we just wanted to ask them some basic questions so we would know what to expect when the other side subpoena's them to court. I would stress the subpoena part and be sure to let them know that they will be called to court to testify without pay should they say the wrong thing. I would then start my line of questioning, asking basically the same questions but with a different lead-in. For instance, these questions were taken right out of this book:

109) Did you ever see or hear any employee threaten to shove the food down a patient's throat if they didn't eat?

110) When the food was served, was it served hot or cold?

111) Were bedsores a problem in your opinion?

112) Did you find many patients who were wet and lying in their own urine?

113)   Did the nursing home have an odor of urine?

114)   Do you recall finding many dried rings on the sheets where the person had obviously laid in their own urine until it had dried?

Now, if I were investigating a situation on behalf of the nursing home, I would ask the same questions a little differently such as:

❖ I know that every employee gets a little tired and cranky from time to time, especially when you have some patients who try to fight you; taking into account these factors, did you ever <u>see</u> an employee try to shove food down a patient's throat for not eating?

❖ I know the facility's food was kind of like being back in school, sometimes you liked what they had and sometimes you didn't, but on a whole, was the food served good and hot?

❖ I know that a patient from time to time is going to have a bedsore, but would you consider it a <u>big</u> problem at the facility?

❖ I know that you were a hard worker and that you couldn't be everywhere at the same time, so was patients laying in their own urine a major problem?

❖ We both know from being around the elderly and hospitals that they have a smell all their own, but do you remember the smell of urine being a problem throughout the facility?

❖ I know that when you are busy you can't change a person right after they wet the bed, but was finding dried urine circles on the sheets a major problem?

You can see that the way the sentence is phrased will have an impact on the answer to the question. This is often called "leading" a witness. This is part of a good interviewer's technique. We are not asking the person to lie or miss-state the facts, we are merely putting a suggestion into their mind that the situation was really worse than they thought it was or it wasn't as bad as they though it was.

Part of defending nursing homes is going to be discrediting possible witnesses. This will mean that the investigator will have to do a general background check on the person's character and moral stability. Although they might have hired a person with a prior problem of abusing people, if you find it first before trial, the attorney will not get blind-sided and may be able to squash the information and keep it out of court.

Unfortunately, at this particular moment in time, the nursing home industry is their own worst enemy. I don't see any major changes in legislation or in industry standards on the horizon. When insurance companies get tired of losing big money from defending non-defendable lawsuits, their underwriting guidelines will grow stricter and the cost of insuring the facilities will go up. Until that time, we all have to watch out for our family members and the helpless!

ABUSE AT IT'S WORSE
Chapter Eighteen

"Nursing home records sought after
woman gets sexual disease"

(San Antonio Express News)

"A lawyer for the family of an 80-year-old woman who contracted a sexually transmitted disease at a nursing home wants her caregivers to turn over the woman's medical records.   The petition states that, while a resident of XXX, the woman "sustained personal injuries which are believed to have been the result of negligence" on the part of the nursing home."

"Nursing Home Supervisor put on probation"
(San Antonio Express News, Aug. 13, 1997)

"A regulatory board criticized for a lack of action took its first disciplinary measure against a nursing home administrator Tuesday...placed an administrator on six months' probation."

"At the same time, the board closed more than 100 cases rather than impose discipline on administrators accused of running problem homes."

The cases involved: An administrator who ran a home where four people died after staff members failed to notify a doctor when the resident's health took a turn for the worse. The XXX nursing home had so many life threatening problems that a trustee had to take over.

An administrator who was accused of running a nursing home where residents had severe bed sores and were bathed only sporadically

Another administrator who was accused of failing to ensure that residents did not wander to a highway or to protect them from assault by other residents

The nursing home administrator who was given a 6 months suspension was cited for:

- Failing to provide a safe, clean environment
- Failing to ensure that resident call systems were functioning adequately
- Failing to ensure the home kept emergency, dangerous drugs in locked storage

---

> "Woman's heirs awarded $92 million in
> nursing home neglect judgment"

(Associated Press, Nov. 9, 1997)

"A jury awarded $92 million in damages to the family of a woman who died in a Ft. Worth nursing home after finding the home's former operators liable for gross neglect. "

"During her 1995 stay at the nursing home, XXX, then in her early 70s, was malnourished, suffered a bedsore on her right hip through which bone could be seen, and contracted into the fetal position."

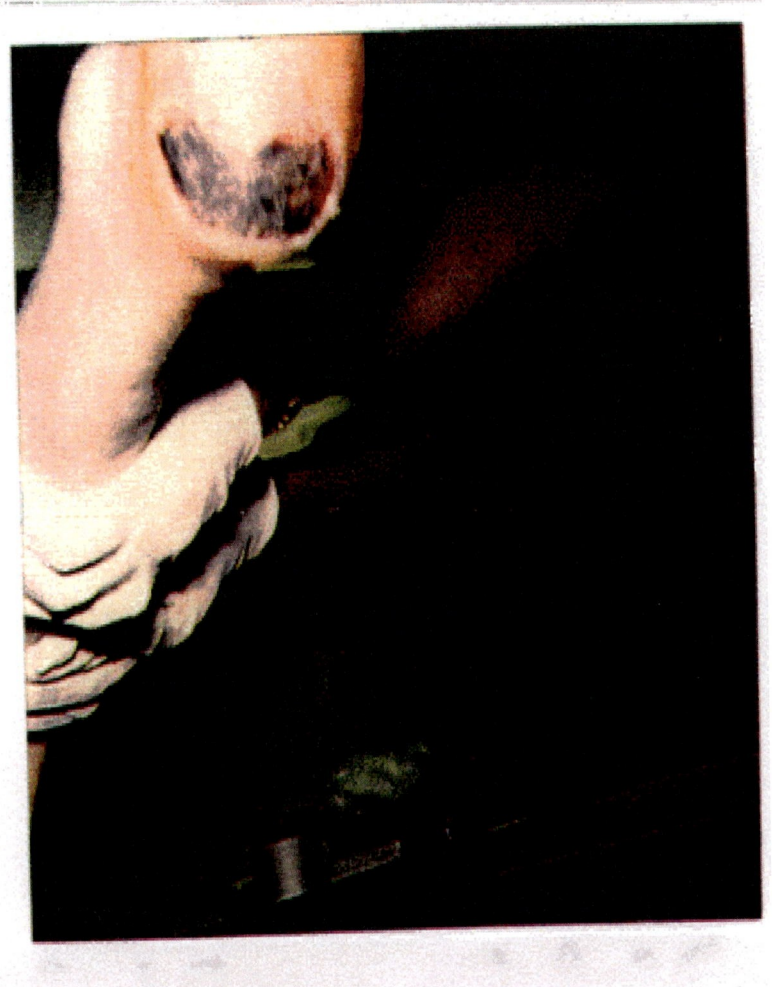

Heel with skin disorder.

"In a recent audit of nursing homes in six states, the Dept. of Health & Human Services discovered that poor background screening programs led to the frequent hire of individuals with criminal histories."

"In the 8 Maryland nursing homes visited, 51 employees, 5% of the total 1,000 employees, had been convicted of a crime. HHS also conducted background checks on 35 people who had been recently convicted of elder abuse in Maryland. Of these, 7 had prior convictions for similar crimes."

"In 1997, the state (Illinois) found that 5% of prospective nursing home employees had committed crimes that would preclude their employment in a nursing home. In addition, the state recommended the termination of 759 certified nurses as a result of the background checks."

"In reviewing a sample of 88 cases of alleged abuse reported by nursing homes, the audit found that the state failed to investigate 13 cases."

"Rules change for reporting malpractice claims"
(Associated Press, Washington)

"Individual physicians and dentists who make payments out of their own pockets to settle patient complaints no longer must report them to a federal data bank."

"The vast majority of malpractice payments are made by insurance companies, hospitals and other health care entities and those settlements will have to be reported to the National Practitioner Data Bank."

"Only 300 of the 90,000 reports in the data bank dealt with payments by individual physicians, dentists and other licensed health care practitioners."

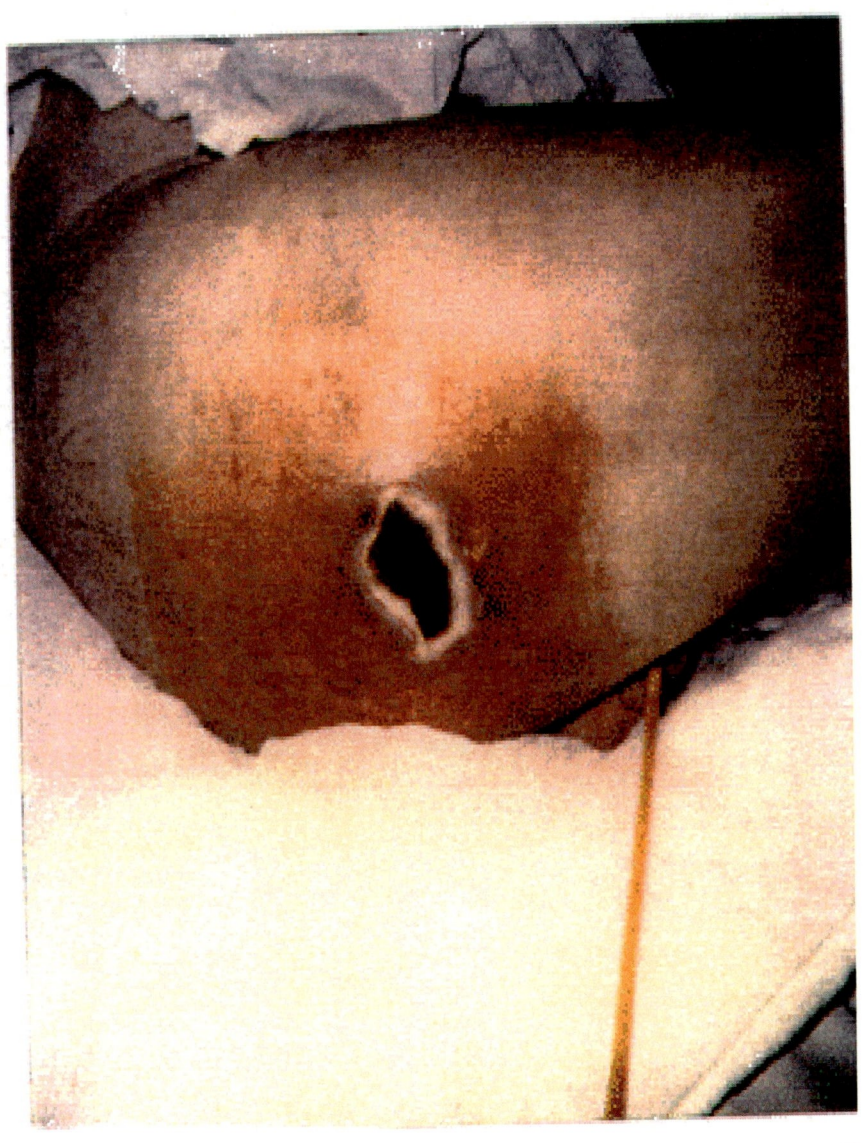

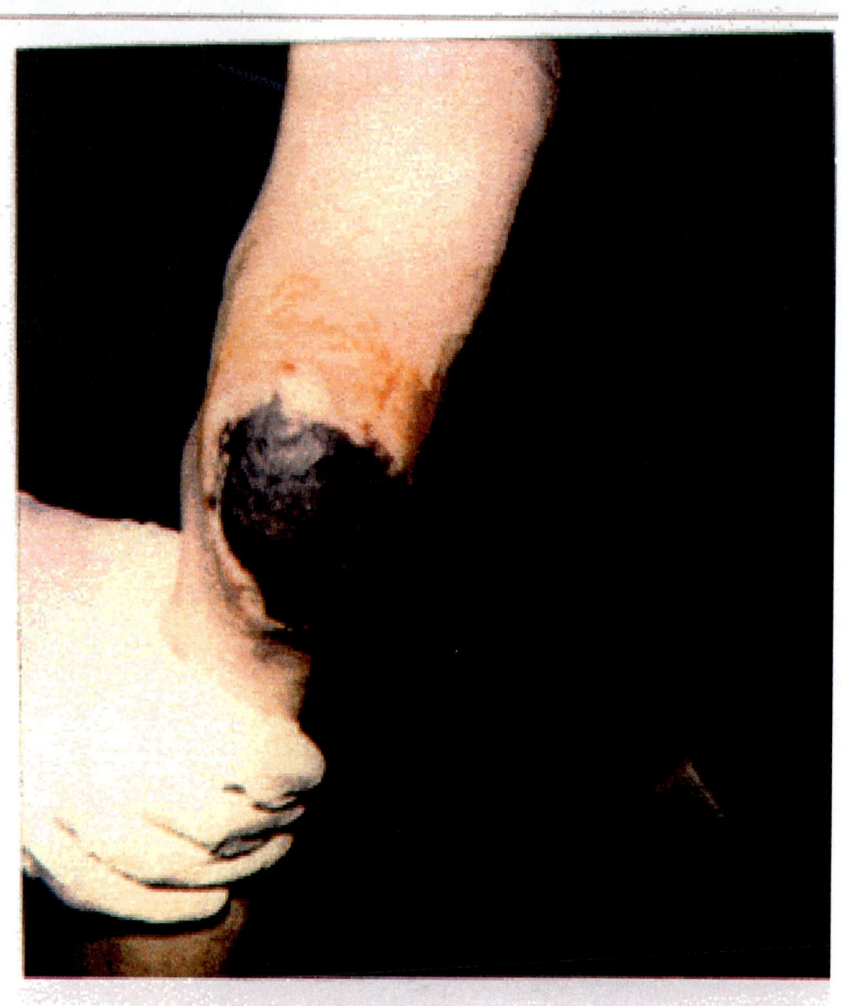

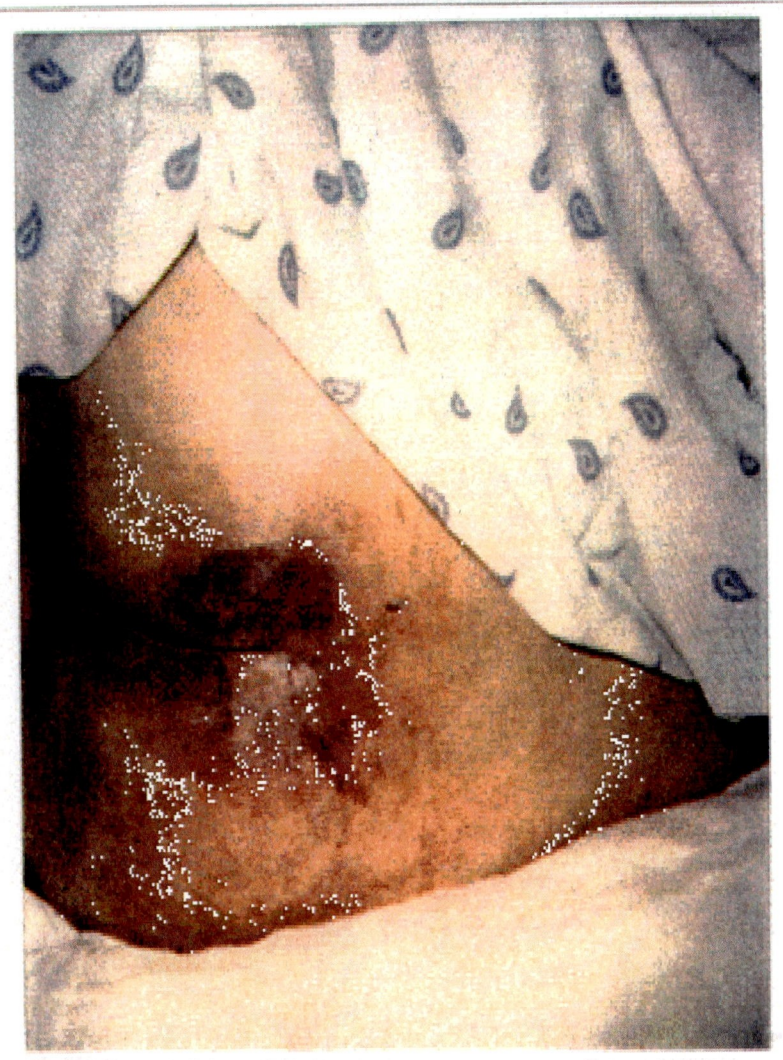

Q: Do you know of any specific situations like bad bedsores or --

A: "As a matter of fact, there was a lady that passed away last week during the time I was on vacation. The girls were telling me that they found maggots in her stump (amputee)."

I said, but how? The nurse said "the leg hasn't been cleaned.

As a matter of fact, the first time we found it, we could smell something horrible. We took off her sock and she had a hole in the side of her foot.

We told the charge nurse and I asked her, "what are they going to do about it? Are they going to send her to the hospital? Are they going to amputate it like her other leg? What's going to happen?"

"Oh no," she said, "she's eventually going to lose it. She's going to get gangrene."

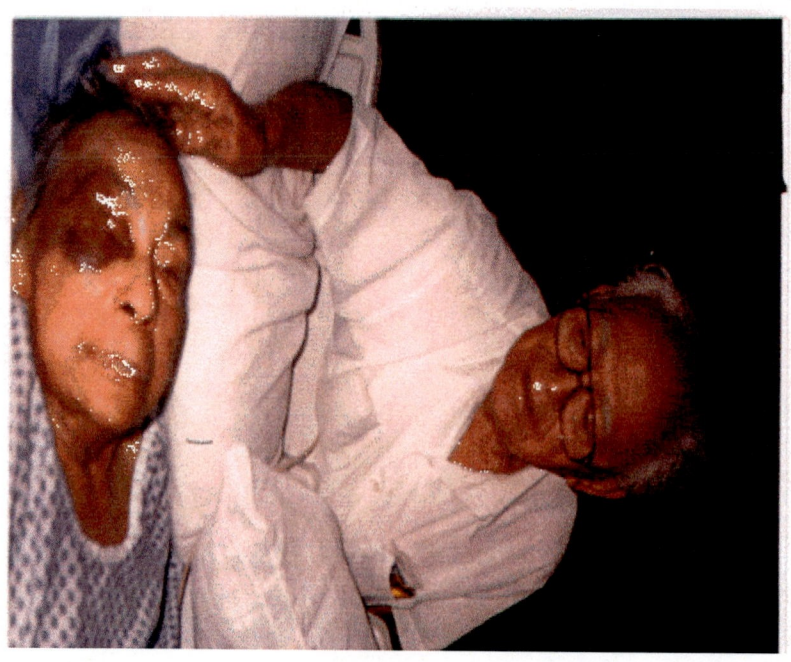

Patient with Black Eye

FINANCIAL ABUSE
Chapter Nineteen

Financial abuse of the elderly or those who have mental illnesses is way too common and easily done by the abuser. The levels of financial abuse vary depending on circumstances, opportunity, illnesses and assets available. Family members of an elderly person living in an assisted living facility will often give the patient access to some funds in the event they want something from the vending machines, etc. Realistically the patient does not need access to cash or any other financial instruments such as a check book or credit card. You will most likely be targeted if the patient has any of this in their room. Caregivers that abuse patients by stealing from them simply blame the patient by indicating they do not remember what they have due to dementia. It is therefore wise not to leave any jewelry or anything else of value with the patient. When they first enter the facility it may be more difficult to get them to part with the items as this appears to be another attempt to take away their freedom and self-reliance.

Elder abuse includes the illegal or improper use of an older adult's funds, property, or assets. Recent studies suggest that financial exploitation is the most rapidly increasing form of elder abuse and that only a small fraction of incidents are reported. Older adults can become targets of financial exploitation by family members, caregivers, scam artists, financial advisers, home repair contractors, fiduciaries (such as agents under power of attorney and guardians), and others. Older adults are attractive targets because they may have significant assets or equity in their homes. They may be especially vulnerable due to isolation, cognitive decline, physical disability, health problems, and/or the recent loss of a partner, family member, or friend.

Caregivers have access to the patient's social security number, date of birth and personal information. With this, they can forge credit card applications and do a great deal of damage financially. It is therefore important to review the patient's credit report yearly and possibly subscribe to a credit watch program.

From a preventative stance, financial institutions can play a key role in preventing and detecting elder financial exploitation. A financial institution's familiarity with older adults it encounters may enable it to spot irregular transactions, account activity, or behavior. Prompt reporting of suspected financial exploitation to adult protective services, law enforcement, and/or long-term care ombudsmens can trigger appropriate intervention, prevention of financial losses, and other remedies.

Common Signs of Financial Abuse Include:

1) Erratic or unusual banking transactions, or changes in banking patterns: Debit transactions that are inconsistent for the older adult; and

2) Frequent large withdrawals, including daily maximum currency withdrawals from an ATM;

3) Sudden non-sufficient fund activity;

4) Uncharacteristic nonpayment for services, which may indicate a loss of funds or access to funds;

5) Uncharacteristic attempts to wire large sums of money; or

6) Closing of CDs or accounts without regard to penalties.

Interactions with older adults or caregivers:

7) A caregiver or other individual shows excessive interest in the older adult's finances or assets, does not allow the older adult to speak for himself, or is reluctant to leave the older adult's side during conversations;

8) The older adult shows an unusual degree of fear or submissiveness toward a caregiver, or expresses a fear of eviction or nursing home placement if money is not given to a caretaker;

9) The financial institution is unable to speak directly with the older adult, despite repeated attempts to contact him or her;

10) A new caretaker, relative, or friend suddenly begins conducting financial transactions on behalf of the older adult without proper documentation;

11) The older adult moves away from existing relationships and toward new associations with other "friends" or strangers;

12) The older adult's financial management changes suddenly, such as through a change of power of attorney to a different family member or a new individual; or

13) The older adult lacks knowledge about his or her financial status, or shows a sudden reluctance to discuss financial matters.

Further information about the use of Suspicious Activity Reports to report suspected elder financial exploitation is available in FinCEN's "The SAR Activity Review" published in May 2013. In addition, if financial institutions or other organizations are interested in raising public awareness among older adults and their caregivers about preventing, identifying, and responding to elder financial exploitation, *Money Smart for Older Adults*, a financial resource tool, serves as a helpful source of training and information.

NOTE: Complete Interagency Guidance on Privacy Laws and Reporting Financial Abuse of Older Adult with footnotes are available at:

http://files.consumerfinance.gov/f/201309_cfpb_elder-abuse-guidance.pdf

As an example of miss-use of a patient's money, as well as poor judgment on the part of a nursing home the following story details the abuse:

Male stripper goes to nursing home, elderly resident's son goes to court

By **Steve Almasy**, CNN
updated 8:10 AM EDT, Wed April 9, 2014

(CNN) -- Somebody at a New York nursing home apparently thought it would be a great idea to bring in a young hard body for the elderly residents to watch dance. In other words, a male stripper.

But after a man found a picture in his 86-year-old mother's belongings of a man wearing only "tighty whiteys" hovering very much in his mom's personal space, the lawyers got involved.

Bernice Youngblood, the wheelchair-bound resident whose son, Franklin, is suing the home on her behalf, told CNN affiliate WCBS, "I felt terrible. I was shaken and going on."

WCBS reported that the East Neck Nursing and Rehabilitation Center in West Babylon said all 16 people on a panel of residents approved the show.

"There is nothing inappropriate about it," the facility's attorney, Howard Fensterman, told reporters on Tuesday. Fensterman, according to the WCBS report, said that Bernice Youngblood enjoyed the event and was chaperoned by her son's live-in girlfriend, who the nursing home said appears in the photo. The family said the woman in the photo is a nursing-home staff member.

According to a lawsuit filed last month, Bernice Youngblood, who the suit says has partial dementia, was "confused and bewildered" when the stripper approached her and directed her to "place her hands about and upon his body, including his genital area."

The suit contends the home has hired male strippers on other occasions for the "perverse pleasure of the defendant's staff."

Franklin Youngblood said his mother was forced to tip the stripper **with her own money, which is supposed to be locked away at the nurses' station.**

"There's too much sex and craziness that's going on. Now they're bringing it to the nursing home, and it don't belong here," he told WCBS. The suit is asking for a financial judgment of unspecified amounts from a jury at trial. It is unclear from the legal documents when the stripping incident occurred.

ADULT DAYCARE CENTERS
Chapter Twenty

Adult day care centers are designed to get the adult out of the house and into an environment where they can enjoy the company of adults in the similar stages of their lives. They provide a planned program of activities designed to promote well-being though social and health-related services. The centers typically operate during daytime hours, Monday through Friday, and include meals and snacks.

According to the National Adult Day Services Association (NADSA)[27], there are currently more than 4,600 adult day care centers in the United States. Each state provides different regulations for the operation of adult day care centers, although NADSA offers some overall guidelines in its Standards and Guidelines for Adult Day Care.

NADSA recommends a minimum staff-to-participant ratio of one to six. This ratio can be even smaller, depending upon the level of participant impairment. If a program serves a large proportion of participants with dementia, for example, the ratio of staff to participants should be closer to one to four.

Some centers will have a nurse on duty, a social worker, Activity Director, as well as support staff that may include kitchen staff, drivers and a secretary. While the centers are not intended for those with severe medical issues, they are designed to give the elderly something to look forward to and to promote a lifestyle that is not stagnating. Many centers will encompass some of the following activities:

- Arts and crafts

- Musical entertainment and sing-a-longs

- Mental stimulation games such as bingo

- Stretching or other gentle exercise

- Discussion groups (books, films, current events)

---

[27] http://nadsa.org/

- Holiday and birthday celebrations

- Local outings

Cases of abuse and neglect in adult daycare facilities may occur due to a lack of staff or having patients that have health issues beyond what the facility should realistically being caring for as a daycare. As an example, an elderly lady had broken the femur in her leg. After the initial healing time frame, the doctor indicated the patient could return to the daycare facility but was not to put any weight on the leg. The patient had a home healthcare employee who wheeled her outside in the wheelchair and assisted as she used the handicap ramp for the facility's bus. At the end of the day, the home healthcare worker was waiting at the street for the return of the patient. The healthcare employee stated that she could hear the patient moaning in pain before the bus even stopped at the house. The patient had on a nice house-dress and the healthcare employee quickly did an assessment. In doing so, she could tell that the femur in the elderly patient's leg was protruding out of her skin.

The follow-up investigation revealed that the patient had been wheeled into the adult daycare facility and placed in view of the T.V. Later in the day, an employee of the facility attempted to move the patient to the sofa. In doing so, she had to stand up and put her weight on the leg. A different employee stated that she heard a popping sound but did not realize it had come from the patient's leg. Instead of getting the patient medical assistance, the employee left the patient who immediately began to moan with discomfort.

With the technology available today, it is recommended that a center be located that provides cameras whereby the family can log into the facility's cameras via the internet. In doing so, the family can keep a checks-and-balances.

The selection process is extremely important and some questions that should be answered include:

- Who owns or sponsors the adult day care center?

- How long has it been operating?

- Is it licensed or certified? (If required in your state)

- What are the days and hours of operation?

- Is transportation to and from the adult day care center provided?

- Which conditions are accepted (e.g., memory loss, limited mobility, incontinence)?

- What are the staff's credentials?

- What activities are offered?

- Are there a variety of individual and group programs?

- Are meals and snacks included?

- Are special diets accommodated?

Through this and a visual inspection you should be able to judge for yourself and determine if the facility is right for you and your family member.

SELECTING A FACILITY
Chapter Twenty-one

Whether you are selecting a nursing home, adult daycare or healthcare facility this is a process and one that requires diligent research. One of the best initial resources is your physician. Additionally, it is important in order to determine which type of licensed care facility you will be seeking, from the Acute Hospital to Sub-acute Skilled Nursing Facility (SNF), Intermediate Care Facility (ICF) or Residential Facility for Elderly (RFE) (more commonly referred to as Board and Care or Retirement Homes). The RFE is for non-medical care and supervision that may include personal services (help in bathing and grooming, guidance in dressing, aid in taking self-administered medications) and help with other daily living activities.

After determining the type of facility and getting any referral from your physician, it now becomes your responsibility to do the proper investigation needed to insure the facility is licensed. There are numerous websites like www.Healthgrades.com that provide a grading system for facilities as well as information about what type of facility they are, how many beds and rooms they have and other useful information.

You should check with the state licensing board to determine any disciplinary issues or fines that may have been given to the facility as well as whether or not they have been resolved.

A check of the District Clerk's records for the county where the facility is located will provide information about lawsuits. A simple internet search will provide the District Clerk's website and many allow the search to be conducted on their website.

Other things to consider include:

Determine your needs

What specific services are important to the person using the center?

- A safe, secure environment?

- Social activities?

- Assistance with daily living skills – walking, eating, taking medications, bathing?

- Therapies – physical, speech, occupational, nursing?

- Health monitoring – blood pressure, blood sugar levels, food/liquid intake, weight?

- Nutritious meals and/or snacks? Special diet?

- Exercise programming?

- Specialized care such as dementia care or TBI care?

What do you, the caregiver need?

- Occasional free time?

- Coverage while working?

- Transportation for your loved one?

- Assistance in planning care?

Locate an adult day center

- Contact your local Area Agency on Aging (800-677-1116)

- Ask at a local senior center or organization serving persons with developmental disabilities (as applicable)

- Use a search engine to locate a center and review center websites

Site Visit - Make an appointment to visit the center(s)

– Check references

- Talk to two or three people who have used the center you are considering. Ask for their opinion.

Determining what is important to you beforehand will enable you to make a more realistic choice and insure that the facility is capable of assisting your needs.

Depending on your situation, it may be appropriate to check with the Fire Department to determine if they have made any calls there and the nature of the calls.

Likewise, it may be appropriate to check with the police department for any police calls associated with the facility. You can usually ask for a list of calls by year at the records department in the main police station.

Conduct an internet search (commonly referred to as a Google search) for any and all information related to the address and the name of the facility. Be sure to search by entering the street address. Conduct a separate search using the facilities name. If you determine the facility is owned by a large company or has any "sister" facilities, you will want to research these names as well as this will give you an indication of their overall culture. You should find positive stories but may find adverse information that would be utilized during the selection process.

You will find the following lists useful and you may want to print these if conducting an evaluation of a facility:

Site Visit Checklist:

Does the exterior appear well kept?   Yes___ No___.

Is the exterior doors locked? Yes___ No___.

Is there video cameras watching the facility? Yes___ No___.

Were you greeted upon entering or allowed to wonder?

Did you feel welcome? Yes___ No___.

Did the interior appear clean? Yes___ No___.

Did the staff have a professional appearance? Yes___ No___.

Were the center services/activities explained? Yes___ No___.

Were you given information regarding staffing? Yes___ No___.

Is the facility free of odor? Yes___ No___.

Is the building and site wheelchair accessible? Yes___ No___.

Is the furniture sturdy and comfortable? Yes___ No___.

Was the facility quiet or in chaos?

Did the sheets, bedding and towels appear clean? Yes___ No___.

Were patients allowed to wonder or sit unattended? Yes___ No___.

Do they have a secure outside courtyard area? Yes___ No___.

Questions to ask when visiting a facility:

How many years has the center been in operation?

Have they recently changed their name?

Does the center have a license, certification and/or accreditation?

Have they had their license suspended or revoked?

What are the hours of operation?

Are transportation services offered?

What is the cost?

Is financial assistance available?

Is specialized care provided (skilled/unskilled nursing)?

What is the staff/ patient ratio?

Is a Registered Nurse always on duty?

What kind of training does staff receive?

Do they do their own training?

Do participants have access to services such as physical or occupational therapy?

What type of activities are provided?

Are meals and/or snacks provided?

Do they have a Dietitian on staff?

Have they ever had any patients wander off unsupervised?

When was their last audit and their score?

There are other resources available to assist you in the selection of a facility including:

Long-Term Care Ombudsman

Long-Term Care Ombudsman are advocates for residents of nursing homes, board and care homes, assisted living facilities, and similar adult care facilities. They work to resolve problems of individual residents and to bring about changes at the local, state, and national levels that will improve residents' care and quality of life.

Duties of Long-Term Care Ombudsman:

- Visit nursing homes and speak with residents throughout the year to make sure residents' rights are protected

- Work to solve problems with your nursing home care, including financial issues

- Discuss general information about nursing homes and nursing home care

- Help you compare a nursing home's strengths and weaknesses

- Answer questions, like how many complaints they've gotten about a specific nursing home, what kind of complaints they were, and if the issues were resolved in a timely manner.

The National Ombudsman Resource Center, which has contact information for States' Long-Term Care Ombudsman Programs can be reached via their website: ltcombudsman.org.

You can also utilize the Eldercare Locator at 1-800-677-1116 to get the phone number for your local ombudsman program office.

Nursing Home Comparison
Medicare's Nursing Home Compare allows you to find and compare information about nursing homes. Their website has more information at: Medicare.gov/nhcompare

Centers for Medicare & Medicaid Services (CMS)

CMS is an agency in the federal government that can give you more information about Medicare and Medicaid coverage, home and community-based services, and other health-related topics. Their website is: Medicare.gov or phone 1-800-633-4227

Centers for Independent Living (CILs)

Centers for Independent Living (CILs) support people with disabilities find community living options and develop independent living skills. Their website is: www.ilru.org/hmlt/publications/directory/index.html.

Quality Improvement Organizations (QIOs)
A QIO is a group of practicing doctors and other health care experts paid by the federal government to check and improve the care given to people with Medicare. Your QIO can help if you have questions or want to report complaints about the quality of your care for a Medicare-covered service or if you think Medicare coverage for your service is ending too soon. For more information: Medicare.gov/contacts, or call 1-800-MEDICARE (1-800-633-4227) to get the phone number for the QIO in your state.

State Health Insurance Assistance Programs (SHIPs)
Your SHIP can give you free health insurance counseling. SHIPs are state programs that get money from the federal government to give free, local

health insurance counseling. More information can be obtained at: Medicare.gov/contacts, or call 1-800-MEDICARE to get the phone number for the SHIP in your state.

The following are check-lists to assist in your evaluation process[28]:

Name of nursing home: _____

Address: _____

Phone number: _____

Date of visit: _____

Basic information	Yes	No
Is the nursing home Medicare-certified?		
Is the nursing home Medicaid-certified?		
Does the nursing home have the level of care I need?		
Does the nursing home have a bed available?		
Does the nursing home offer specialized services, like a special unit for care for a resident with dementia, ventilator care, or rehabilitation services?		
Is the nursing home located close enough for friends and family to visit?		

[28] http://www.medicare.gov/Publications/Pubs/pdf/02174.pdf

Resident appearance	Yes	No
Are the residents clean, well groomed, and appropriately dressed for the season or time of day?		
Nursing home living spaces	**Yes**	**No**
Is the nursing home free from overwhelming unpleasant odors?		
Does the nursing home appear clean and well kept?		
Is the temperature in the nursing home comfortable for residents?		
Does the nursing home have good lighting?		
Are the noise levels in the dining room and other common areas comfortable?		
Is smoking allowed? If so, is it restricted to certain areas of the nursing home?		
Are the furnishings sturdy, yet comfortable and attractive?		

Residents' rooms	Yes	No
Can residents have personal belongings and furniture in their rooms?		
Does each resident have storage space (closet and drawers) in his or her room?		
Does each resident have a window in his or her bedroom?		
Do residents have access to a personal phone and television?		
Do residents have a choice of roommates?		
Are there policies and procedures to protect residents' possessions, including lockable cabinets and closets?		

Hallway, stairs, lounges, and bathrooms	Yes	No
Are exits clearly marked?		
Are there quiet areas where residents can visit with friends and family?		
Does the nursing home have smoke detectors and sprinklers?		
Are all common areas, resident rooms, and doorways designed for wheelchair use?		
Are handrails and grab bars appropriately placed in the hallways and bathrooms?		

Menus & food	Yes	No
Do residents have a choice of food items at each meal? (Ask if your favorite foods are served.)		
Can the nursing home provide for special dietary needs (like low-salt or no-sugar-added diets)?		
Are nutritious snacks available upon request?		
Does the staff help residents eat and drink at mealtimes if help is needed?		

Activities	Yes	No
Can residents, including those who are unable to leave their rooms, choose to take part in a variety of activities?		
Do residents have a role in planning or choosing activities that are available?		
Does the nursing home have outdoor areas for resident use? Is the staff available to help residents go outside?		
Does the nursing home have an active volunteer program?		

Safety & care	Yes	No
Does the nursing home have an emergency evacuation plan and hold regular fire drills (bed-bound residents included)?		
Do residents get preventive care, like a yearly flu shot, to help keep them healthy? Does the facility assist in arranging hearing screenings or vision tests?		
Can residents still see their personal doctors? Does the facility help in arranging transportation for this purpose?		
Does the nursing home have an arrangement with a nearby hospital for emergencies?		
Are care plan meetings held with residents and family members at times that are convenient and flexible whenever possible?		
Has the nursing home corrected all deficiencies (failure to meet one or more state or Federal requirements) on its last state inspection report?		

INDEX

ABOUT THE AUTHOR

<u>Professional Experience Narrative:</u>   Mr. Riddle has more than 35 years of investigative experience and earned a Bachelor of Science degree in Criminal Justice from the University of North Alabama. He was chosen as the **"PI of the Year"** by the National Association of Investigative Specialists and the PI Magazine named Mr. Riddle as the **"#1 PI in the United States"**. He has been designated an expert in surveillance, insurance investigations, nursing home abuse and computer investigations. He was chosen as **"One of the Top 25 PI's of the 20th Century."**   Kelly obtained his **Texas Certified Investigator** designation (less than 50 in TX.) Mr. Riddle is also the past **President (2010-2012) for TALI** - the Texas Association of Licensed Investigators (TALI); **Board of Directors (2007-2010) for TALI** as well as being on the Board of Directors for the **Freedom of Information Foundation of Texas**. Kelly is on the Public Relations committee for the **Council of International Investigators** and the Membership Chair for the San Antonio Chapter of ASIS. He is a Founding Board Member and Board Advisor for the non-profit organization "Can You Identify Me." Kelly was the recipient of the **2013 Hudgins-Sallee award**, the highest recognition presented by the Texas Association of Licensed Investigators.

Mr. Riddle is the author of 10 books and has published more than 40 articles. He has been the guest speaker at more than 400 events and has been on national TV, radio and newspapers.

Prior law enforcement experience includes being a member of the SWAT team, a Training Officer, Emergency Medical Technician, Evidence Technician, Arson Investigator, Juvenile Specialist and Traffic Investigator.

Mr. Riddle is the Founder and President of the **PI Institute of Education**, as well as the **Association of Christian Investigators** with more than 1000 members in the U.S. and 19 countries. Kelly is the Founder of the **Coalition of Association Leaders** comprised of past and present board members from state, national and international associations.

Mr. Riddle is a member of NAIS,TALI,ASIS,NALI,FAPI,LAPI, USAPI,ACI, NAAA,PICA,WIN, NLLI, CTIB, CLEAR,IOPIA,TIDA,CII,ASSIST

For more information, please review our websites at www.kelmarpi.com, www.a-c-i.com and www.PIinstitute.com. You may reach Mr. Riddle via the Internet at the e-mail address of Kelly@KelmarGlobal.com.

 Kelly E. Riddle

Other Products by Kelly E. Riddle

➢ Book: "Private Investigating Made Easy"

➢ Book: "Insurance Investigations from A to Z"

➢ Book: "The Art of Surveillance"

➢ Book: "Security Consulting for the 21st Century Consultant"

➢ Book: "Exposed – True Cases of America's #1 PI"

➢ Book: "The Internet Black Book"

22866955R00083

Made in the USA
San Bernardino, CA
24 July 2015